Wisdom
of the Heart

MAHANTA

This book has been authored by and published under the supervision of the Mahanta, the Living ECK Master, Sri Harold Klemp. It is the Word of ECK.

Wisdom
of the Heart

Book 1

HAROLD KLEMP

ℰ𝕂

ECKANKAR
Minneapolis

Wisdom of the Heart, Book 1

Copyright © 1992 ECKANKAR

The terms ECKANKAR, ECK, EK, MAHANTA, SOUL TRAVEL, and VAIRAGI, among others, are trademarks of ECKANKAR, P.O. Box 27300, Minneapolis, MN 55427 U.S.A.

Printed in U.S.A.

Compiled by Mary Carroll Moore
Edited by Joan Klemp and Anthony Moore
Cover photo by Bernard Chouet
Illustrations by Catherine Purnell

Third Printing—2004

Publisher's Cataloging-in-Publication
(Provided by Quality Books, Inc.)

Klemp, Harold.
    Wisdom of the heart. Book 1 / Harold Klemp.
    p. cm.
    Includes bibliographical references and index.
    LCCN 2004108400
    ISBN 1-57043-209-0

    1. Eckankar (Organization) 2. Love. 3. Spiritual life—
Eckankar (Organization)   I. Title.

BP605.E3K54 2004   299'.93
                                            QBI33-2088

∞ The paper used in this publication meets the minimum requirements of the American National Standard for Information Sciences —Permanence of Paper for Printed Library Materials, ANSI Z39.48-1984.

CONTENTS

Chapter Twelve: Going Home to God

FOREWORD

The Wisdom Notes are letters from the Living ECK Master to the chelas of ECK. Published in the *Mystic World*, each letter speaks to timely spiritual issues—the problem of agitation, how to find success in ECK, how to weather tests and unexpected change, and how to move beyond your own inner experiences.

If you read these letters carefully, highlighting the passages that speak to your heart, you may notice the effect of their rhythm on your life. The Wisdom Notes can bring important insights and show you ways to navigate the rough spots on your own spiritual journey.

The Vairagi Adepts give special wisdom and knowledge to those who have dedicated themselves to ECK. When one dedicates himself in this way through membership in Eckankar, a vital communication link with the Mahanta, the Living ECK Master is opened. His Wisdom Notes are but one of the ways he uses to guide Soul home to God.

The loaded wheelbarrow was like the karmic load that people haul around with them everywhere they go. If the construction worker had wanted to change his life, he could have begun to sing HU, a love song to God.

CHAPTER ONE

Changing Your Life

1
WHAT'S THE LESSON HERE?

*I*n these Wisdom Notes I am able to talk more informally with you, without always having to follow a tight structure. This time I would like to speak on the range of experience, from the simplest to the more encompassing. The binding agent is finally seen to be the HU.

An old friend of an ECKist is a construction worker, and an alcoholic. At least once a month he swears he'll never drink again, only to go back on his word within a few days or weeks. Although the construction worker is not a member of Eckankar, the experience that befell him was not lost upon the ECK initiate.

The construction worker was in a huge parking garage that was being built in the downtown area. All day long he had been cleaning up the site using a massive, bulky, motorized wheelbarrow. Loading it up with wood, concrete, and other trash, he would take it down the ramps to the Dumpster outside. But the routine made him careless. Instead of walking down a ramp behind the cart, he began to walk in front of it. Becoming even more careless, he started weaving back and forth with it—to break

In these Wisdom Notes I am able to talk more informally with you on the range of experience, from the simplest to the more encompassing.

3

the monotony. Accidentally, he bumped the gear-shift lever and knocked it into neutral. The wheel-barrow had no brakes. It picked up speed so fast there was no time to turn around and relock the shift lever into gear to stop it. Frantically he ran down the ramp to keep ahead of the rolling machine, trying not to get crushed under its wheels. Something told him he had but one chance: to dive off to the side. He barely made it, getting nicked in the heel by the machine's wheels before it went crashing into a concrete pillar at the bottom of the ramp.

The worker told the ECKist he had never been so frightened in his life. "Do you see the spiritual lesson?" asked the chela. The worker quickly changed the subject.

The ECKist saw the experience as if it were a dream. The loaded wheelbarrow was the karmic load that people haul around with them everywhere they go. In the construction worker's case, he was going in circles, repeating the same cycles year after year. Many people, when something drastic or painful happens to them, make a resolution to straighten up and change their course in life—going upward toward God and a greater life. But in most cases they fail to let go of their habits or burdens. Thus they do not drop the karmic load, but continue to drag it along behind them.

Now I would like to skip on to the HU chant. If the construction worker had wanted to change his life, he could have begun to sing this love song to God. Through it, one is lifted into a higher spiritual realm and becomes able to serve mankind in interesting and shining ways. But the purpose of the HU chant is hard for some to understand.

Through the HU chant, this love song to God, one is lifted into a higher spiritual realm and becomes able to serve mankind in interesting and shining ways.

A young man in Germany had a difficult time in seeing its meaning until he had a wonderful dream. He and his girlfriend came to visit an Italian family. They were there for only one reason: The grandmother was near death and the Mahanta told them to go to her bedside. The old woman said to them, "I want to leave, but somehow cannot. I know the Mahanta has brought you." Suddenly, without a second thought, he and his girlfriend began to chant HU. And as they chanted softly, the grandmother of this family they had come to visit in the dream state began to leave her body in total peace and without fear. It was the dreamer's first real understanding of the HU chant as the true love song for God, or Sugmad.

On the historical side, an ECKist who has studied a collection of Coptic texts known as the Nag Hammadi Library learned something of interest to ECK initiates. The texts of the Nag Hammadi Library are mostly fourth-century copies of earlier Greek versions. The original texts were based upon the inner experiences of the Gnostics. In those first three hundred years of the Christian church, however, the outer path had lost the inner journeys of Soul. All that remained were degenerated myths that reduced earlier spiritual experiences into nothing more than allegories.

In his research, this ECK initiate found a dimension to the original biblical teachings that has been lost in today's church. In the *Marsanes*, a fragmentary codex, there is a guide to thirteen planes and a discussion of sound keys to the planes and luminaries of those planes. *The Paraphrase of Shem* talks of inner travel as the mind's separation from the body, "as if in sleep." Another text, *The*

In those first three hundred years the Christian church had lost the inner journeys of Soul.

Apocalypse of Paul, tells of Paul's heavenly journeys and his transformation upon reaching the tenth heaven. But it is *The Discourse on the Eighth and the Ninth* which is most interesting for us. It gives a hermetic exercise for travel to purely spiritual planes, including chanting a secret "name" that can be transliterated from the original Coptic as—HU.

The Gnostics were people whose spiritual path was an inner one. Unfortunately, they did not balance it with a strong outer path, which is why they succumbed to the institutional church of orthodoxy. Therefore, the secret name of God which had been set into their midst by Zadok was eventually lost.

The future of Eckankar could hold the potential for a repeat of those early times. The difference between us and the Gnostics, however, is that we must be sensible enough to keep a balance between the inner and outer teachings—giving the needed attention to both. Unless this balance is maintained, there is but a broken, one-sided path that cannot truly minister to the spiritual needs of people.

At the heart of our future in ECK is the HU— the ancient love song to God.

We must keep a balance between the inner and outer teachings—giving the needed attention to both.

2
Your Spiritual Thirst

The subject of how to quench one's spiritual thirst touches the basics of the ECK teachings. During the Christmas season "the holiday blues" push past all the partying and revelry and leave a lingering sadness that we don't find peace with God in a crowd.

At issue is our native attitude: How little can I give of myself and still get the greatest return from God? The only food that satisfies spiritual hunger in the struggling is the Sound and Light of God.

In *Stranger by the River*, by Paul Twitchell, Rebazar Tarzs cautions the seeker to solve the mystery of the little self before tackling the mystery of God. Given a choice, the human consciousness prefers power to the chance to find the inner temple. Does gossip still appeal to you? Are the faults of others greater than your own? Is it easier to fix blame on the other fellow or your spouse when things go wrong? That's the little self. Soul's only goal is to love God and find It as your own self.

Spiritual thirst is the divine urge that always nudges Soul toward God. Surrender of the little self

The only food that satisfies spiritual hunger is the Sound and Light of God.

to the Mahanta is the only way to gain love and wisdom. The sure way to do this is by the Spiritual Exercises of ECK done faithfully, on a regular basis. The personal word, the sacred prayer song, must be sung with a sweet love for God. It will not work if there is fear and doubt troubling the heart.

The answer to every question you have about loneliness, guilt, and fear is given in the books and discourses of ECK.

The obstacles of life must be taken as stepping-stones for spiritual development. The answer to every question you have about loneliness, guilt, and fear is given in the books and discourses of ECK. A helpful practice is to read, at bedtime, a short passage from *The Shariyat-Ki-Sugmad.* The golden words therein tune us in to the greater awareness before contemplation and sleep. This time is holy, for we approach the gates that guard the inner worlds.

"The whole of life," said Rebazar Tarzs, "is the appeasement of spiritual hunger, and the infinite states of the world are purely a means of satisfying that hunger." Fulfilling these states actually urges Soul on to higher levels of experience.

Thus we look toward our responsibility to Sugmad, the ECK, the Mahanta, our families, and our neighbors. The purpose of Soul's incarnation, you must remember, is purely to work with God through ECK. An individual or an ECK community may succumb to the little self. Signs of this spiritual introversion are people disputing the direction from the ECK leadership. Yet all the area initiates plan together to work more effectively, spreading the responsibilities of opening ECK centers and bringing the message to the non-initiates. Other signposts of this introversion are backbiting and gossip, less people coming to the introductory lectures.

The reason harmony is so important among the

initiates is that the silent community of seekers senses disruption and arguments among the chosen people. Thoughts are things! And you must never forget this: You are the chosen people. The curious will go elsewhere to find nourishment to quench their spiritual thirst.

As the ECK initiate advances in his unfoldment, he develops a keen insight and perception into life. When he begins to see glimpses of his future, he puts all into the hands of Spirit. He learns that a gift greater than knowledge is the gift of love. The presence of the Mahanta becomes a living reality. He knows the meaning of the statement from the Light Giver, "I am always with you." His heart is filled with the divine food of the Word of God.

When we give up attachment to everything, including the little self, then we find wisdom, power, and freedom!

The presence of the Mahanta becomes a living reality. The ECK initiate knows the meaning of the statement from the Light Giver, "I am always with you."

3

WHY SOUL IS IN
THE LOWER WORLDS

*I*t was heartening to get a letter from an ECKist who has made a profound realization of truth for herself. "Truth is not in the heights but at the bottom of all things," says *The Shariyat-Ki-Sugmad*. "It must be struggled for and sought after and come upon through earnest effort."

For years, this woman had been burdened with an inner tension. She expected that someone, at some time, would tell her that she was doing everything wrong. This made her nervous around Higher Initiates. Recently, Divine Spirit brought her into a situation where the terrible tension was lifted from her. She gained the realization of individual freedom as well as the enormous responsibility to herself.

She met an ECKist who was a stranger to her and asked him if he only drank water. The ECKist looked at her and said gently, full of confidence, "Don't ask me any questions." This hit home. "At that point," she noted, "the mold was destroyed and Light penetrated my consciousness. I finally realized that no one had the right to invade my privacy or my space, that I was allowed to be as individual

"Truth is not in the heights but at the bottom of all things," says *The Shariyat-Ki-Sugmad.* "It must be struggled for and sought after and come upon through earnest effort."

11

as I liked." She felt grateful that the ECK had placed that individual in her path so that she could learn this sense of freedom from fear.

During the Great Depression of the 1930s, President Roosevelt made the now-famous statement, "The only thing we have to fear is fear itself." This is an important point, for those who are bold, those who are courageous will meet God. Those who are timid will never see the face of the Sugmad.

When we first step onto the path of ECK, our motives may be anything other than spiritual unfoldment. A young man approached Sudar Singh and asked to study at his ashram. Sudar Singh asked, "What do you expect to learn from my teaching?" The fellow said, "I want to learn how to get rich!" The ECK Master replied, "I can't help you. All I can do is show you God." The young man did not believe him and announced he would stay anyway. After some months of being in the presence of the Master, and being taken out nightly in the dream state, the young man's goals gradually changed. He gave up his ambitions to learn ways of making money and acquiring all the things that money could buy. His goal now had become Self-Realization, God-Realization, and entering into the kingdom of heaven in this lifetime. Results do not come without true effort.

He knew an individual had to be bold and adventuresome to enter into the Kingdom of God, yet his old ways stated the meek shall inherit the earth. What did this mean?

Another chela was reflecting upon a dilemma: He knew an individual had to be bold and adventuresome to enter into the Kingdom of God, yet his old ways, the teachings of Christianity, stated that the meek shall inherit the earth. What did this mean? "Then while driving it dawned on me what Jesus meant by such a statement," he writes. "Not that the meek will gain control of the earth but,

rather, the meek will be bound to the earth and
never rise into the Kingdom of God."

It is the purpose of the Kal Niranjan to keep
Soul in ignorance of Its true glory. Soul is redeemed
by the Mahanta, for no other being can give one this
true freedom. The spiritual student finds that true
liberation comes with the Master, the initiation,
and the Sound Current. This, says *The Shariyat-Ki-
Sugmad*, is "the truth of the whole purpose of the
Sugmad for Soul's existence in the lower worlds."

*The spiritual
student finds
that true
liberation
comes with
the Master,
the initiation,
and the
Sound Current.*

4
WHAT KEEPS YOU FROM GOD

This month I want to address two spiritual flaws that bother some of you: agitation and drinking alcohol.

Every so often, someone tells me about the misdeeds of another. "Don't you know that so-and-so is a vile wretch who commits such and such foul deeds?" My usual response is: "If you have proof of these allegations, go to the authorities."

Who among you has not returned to earth to repay your karmic debts? The history of our planet is proof enough that earth is full of imperfect beings. As the Living ECK Master, my role in the spiritual works is to be a Wayshower. Someone else is the Lord of Karma. So I leave people alone, for each must learn his own lessons. However, there is an exception to my policy of noninterference: When the selfish or thoughtless acts of some cause others to stumble on the path to God, I give fair warning.

People often see my decision to stand back from the many complaints that come to me as a sign of weakness. Yet, spiritual law holds me to certain duties. My first and only concern is to help people enter the Kingdom of God during this lifetime. My

As the Living ECK Master, my role in the spiritual works is to be a Wayshower. My first and only concern is to help people enter the Kingdom of God during this lifetime.

15

only reason to upset the scheme of cause and effect is to clear unnecessary stumbling blocks from your path to God.

A problem going around lately like a spiritual virus is agitation. That means, to let someone or something trouble your mental, emotional, or physical self too much. One who displays it has lost control of the events in his life. This is nothing to be ashamed of, because life is always doing that to us. Whenever we snuggle into our comfortable nests, it pushes us out into the unknown so we may unfold. We, in our human state of consciousness, rebel at that. Why do others always rob us of our peace of mind?

ECK chelas have the same day-to-day problems as other people. However, the Mahanta comes to them in various ways to help conquer whatever holds them back inside. He ties together the loose ends of an experience, so the individual sees the spiritual harm he does to himself.

An ECK initiate and her husband returned home from an ECK seminar, hoping to continue the peacefulness from the weekend. However, a message on the answering machine said her grandmother had just died. Relatives from out of town were coming to stay with them.

Their home became the headquarters for funeral arrangements. The wife felt bombarded. All the peace and quiet of the ECK seminar had evaporated with the arrival of their guests. The funeral forced her to attend family gatherings she would normally have avoided. On top of everything, her grandmother's death came right at the end of a project the wife had given much time to for a year. The funeral meant missing the awards celebration,

A problem going around like a spiritual virus is agitation. That means, to let someone or something trouble your mental, emotional, or physical self too much.

the dinner, and the dancing. Finally, her relatives left.

However, when they had left, her husband's relatives came to spend the remainder of the week. After they had gone, she felt drained. She wondered how she'd ever reach the Fifth, or Soul, Plane if she couldn't even handle one week of company. That week, her turmoil had hit a peak.

A week later, she had a dream. In it, a messenger of the Mahanta, the Living ECK Master handed her a note that read: "Your agitation is a defect."

Upon awakening, she remained puzzled about the dream all morning. Finally, she looked up *agitate* in the dictionary. She then realized that the message meant this: Her excessive turmoil over the past week was a spiritual weakness. It was keeping her from the God Worlds. Indeed, the Master's use of the word *defect* was an important part of the message. As Soul, we are complete and perfect. Yet, our mind and emotions cannot be that, any more than our physical self can.

From her dream, she also realized the folly of trying to reach complete holiness on earth. She realized it's better to focus on spiritual unfoldment and put her energy to a good, fulfilling use.

Who can fully be rid of a shortcoming, like too much agitation, through a force of will? The Mahanta, the Living ECK Master knows every smudge in one's lower selves. If the chela allows, the Master will gather all his soiled linen of karma and help clean it.

If the chela allows, the Master will gather all his soiled linen of karma and help clean it.

The other cause for concern this month is the habit some have of drinking alcohol. Your desire to have God Consciousness must be true, for It avoids those bedimmed by wine, beer, or liquor.

Alcohol lowers one's state of consciousness. Since the teachings of ECK are all about reaching God Awareness, one hurts himself by having a need for alcohol.

Yes, I know who these people are. But why judge them when they judge themselves? Again, who is to say that one person's craving for alcohol is worse than another's lust for gossip, anger, or deceit? Have you ever noticed that when someone loses himself to any one of these perversions of the mind, he is also out of balance with several more?

Why let your lack of spiritual discipline throw someone else off the path to God? If that happens, part of the debt is yours.

I discourage the use of alcohol. However, if you must drink, do it at home. Think twice before you drink in front of other chelas or in public at ECK seminars. Why let your lack of spiritual discipline throw someone else off the path to God? If that happens, part of the debt is yours. You may think your ECK leadership responsibilities remain as before, but you are slowly losing them. A year or two may pass before it shows outwardly, but the end will come. Should anyone cause another to leave the path to God, he cannot hope to escape his fate.

Use prudence with your defects—and I love you with or without them. However, I also love those whom you injure by your thoughtless deeds. The Law of ECK binds me to protect them.

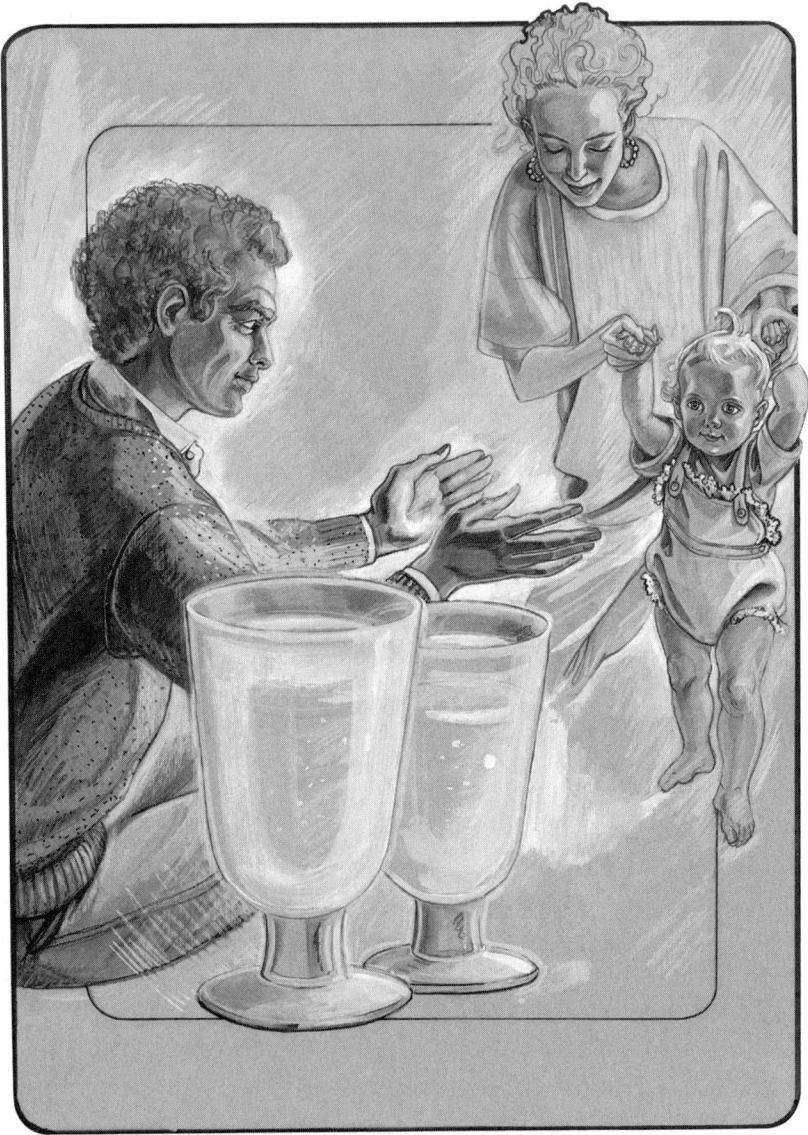

If a karmic relationship is like water from one glass poured half into another, a spiritual one is like two full glasses of water that stand side by side.

CHAPTER TWO

Lessons about Love

5
LOVE'S DIFFERENT LEVELS

*L*ove has been on my mind. Elusive, sensitive, easily misunderstood, it is nevertheless the food of life, without which none of us could live.

Two people who love each other are in ECK—meaning, in the spiritual life—whether or not they are members of Eckankar, the organization. Love is a concrete thing to them: the ECK Current, coming down through the planes to the emotional body, is felt like a touch of another's hand. How can one mistake the concrete reality of the touch of a hand? Nor can the touch of the ECK be mistaken when It passes from the heart of one to the other.

Human love that is of a spiritual nature, instead of karmic, is sustenance for the individuals. It is God's love among mankind.

Many of the relationships mistaken for love are karmic bonds in which the two people are like water from one glass poured half into another. The relationship leaves each only half-full. Life pulls a spiritual being back and forth from one pole to the other: positive to negative, and back again. The movement between the two poles induces Soul to generate Its

Human love that is of a spiritual nature, instead of karmic, is sustenance for the individuals. It is God's love among mankind.

23

creativity, to meet the tests of the hour. So one who is a great seeker of God will be flayed by life, then have a healing oil poured upon his wounds. Each time Soul emerges more pure than before.

Soul matures through shocks to Its lower bodies. Each shock leaves It in a changed state of consciousness. When Soul is in a bond of love, each shock of pain or misunderstanding either widens or narrows Its relationship with the human mate. These shocks are powerful currents that give a strong jolt to a person. And they leave scars. Like scarred tissue, they can become less sensitive and flexible. If there is an increase in sensitivity, often it is to pain rather than to a return of love that is given to one.

Each jolt shuts down the corridors of love along which the ECK comes into each individual, and so, without the essential inflow of the Sound and Light at levels both are used to receiving, the couple begin to drift apart.

If the drifting apart has taken place with one mate, in a karmic rather than a spiritual relationship, ingrained habits will tend to cause all future relationships to follow the same course. Those in the human states of consciousness love their little, peculiar habits because they are as familiar as their own skin—taken for granted. But the habits, if repeated, cause the same breakups as before.

What has been said so far relates to those who are in the human consciousness. If a karmic bond is like water from one glass poured half into another, then a spiritual one is like two full glasses of water that stand side by side.

But yet, the deepest secrets of the loving heart are with the ECK, never with even the beloved.

If a karmic bond is like water from one glass poured half into another, then a spiritual one is like two full glasses of water that stand side by side.

Because these secrets are too refined for words to tell. Thus, the more highly unfolded an individual is, the more lonely he is bound to be at times, because his primary relationship is with the Sound and Light of ECK. All others are secondary. Secondary relationships, though dear ones, cannot know the most secret things of the heart. Only the Mahanta knows.

So where does this leave us? Soul's primary relationship is with the ECK and with the Mahanta. It is through that dual channel that spiritual freedom is found. As one rises through the spiritual planes, his love for the Sugmad becomes everything to him, and because it does, his love for his loved ones and all living things increases in like manner.

Love is the goal, then, of our spiritual search. If it is for any of the lower things—power, influence, control, prestige—they must first pass away through the fires of existence before the individual can rise into the high states of spiritual realization.

The way to God is ever within the heart, within the loving heart.

An initiate who loves the ECK greatly reported having a hard time with the spiritual exercises. This relates to the loving heart, because mental things try to get in the way between Soul and Its destination: the God realm.

Here is her problem: "Whenever I give myself suggestions to stay alert while Soul traveling before I go to sleep," she said, "physical sensations pull me instantly back into my body. I feel very itchy, and this disturbance will continue for some time."

The result of this interference was that she was failing at a particular spiritual exercise. She saw part of the reason for this disturbance, for she

The way to God is ever within the heart, within the loving heart.

continues: "I feel that my subconscious mind is interfering with this natural process by sending me these sensations. But I do not know why it is doing this, nor how to heal myself of it. Inevitably I assume it's karma, which I have no power over, and become passive and helpless."

Our resistance to a disturbance can itself form a mental pattern that automatically calls up the disturbance, as does her spell of itching. Rather than trying to overcome the itching by willpower, it is better to placate the mind and rub the area that is causing the distraction. Let that be the spiritual exercise for several weeks: being aware of all the places in the body that are uncomfortable or distracting, then doing what is required to ease the discomfort.

The subconscious resistance will subside in time, and you will be able to go about the spiritual exercise without interruption.

6
HOW LOVE
ENTERS THE HEART

The central teaching of ECK is love, and we come back to that theme again and again. New members may sometimes find their lives unsettled during their early years in ECK because of spiritual changes taking place within them. However, if you continue with this most direct path to God, you will rise into a state of ecstasy and love during this life.

Divine love enters the heart in a direct line from the Light and Sound of God. Those who become open channels for these twin blessings of ECK will shine with the certainty of life. Even those outside of Eckankar will see this confidence, which radiates like a sunbeam dancing among the roses. What identifies those who have felt the bittersweet kiss of God? The following story will help you recognize them. Even better, you may see yourself.

A while ago, a Higher Initiate named Mark was to teach an ECK Satsang class; no one came. As he sat alone, he reflected upon how casually many people take this teaching of ECK. It interests them, but it only plays a small role in their lives. Then Mark began to wonder, *Who cares? Who really cares*

Divine love enters the heart in a direct line from the Light and Sound of God. Those who become open channels for these twin blessings of ECK will shine with the certainty of life.

if this teaching lives or dies? A few thousand people among the billions, a few dozen books among millions, a small, out-of-the-way teaching. Who would miss it, and who would care?

Then Mark realized, *he* would care if the teachings of ECK were gone. Why? They had been the core of his life for so long: why he breathes and why his heart beats. He cares deeply and passionately for ECK. It is a part of him. Without ECK, there is nothing.

Later, Mark was sharing that insight with someone new to the teachings of ECK. This seeker, still cautious in looking at them, showed Mark another side of what it means to be a Co-worker with God. He also gave Mark a better idea of the responsibilities of a Higher Initiate.

"Never give up this thing called ECK," the seeker said to Mark. "I see you like a ferryman, helping others across the river. You have connections on the inner and the outer, connections the rest of us are trying to make. People will be attracted to you for what you are." Then Mark more fully realized the responsibility of being an ECKist.

Love comes to those who serve God. The rest will look in vain for it.

Love comes to those who serve God. The rest will look in vain for it.

A certain Regional ECK Spiritual Aide is another who has found joy in serving ECK. He made this discovery after three hard years of learning his RESA duties. With misgivings, he decided to give ECK introductions in remote towns in his area. In one place, over thirty people came to a worship service to hear about ECK. That gave him courage to do more. So he went into contemplation to ask the Mahanta for guidance and received a wealth of ideas. Now, when making plans for an introduction on ECK, the RESA puts himself in the seeker's place. He tries to imagine what the individual wants to see or know about ECK. How can he answer the seeker's unspoken question: What's in this for me?

One day, the RESA had a sudden realization: He was in love with life. This change had taken place naturally over the past eight to ten months while his attention was on serving ECK. Someone looking at him might find him little different from before, except now he is perhaps more cheerful, more helpful, and more happy to be alive.

How can he answer the seeker's unspoken question: What's in this for me?

The two ECK initiates mentioned above are finding the wonders of God's love, which has no conditions. Another ECKist, whom we'll call Nancy, is learning that too. A short time ago she awoke from a dream, giddy with excitement. At first, she couldn't remember the dream, but then it slowly came back. While traveling in the other worlds, she had met the ECK Master Fubbi Quantz.

"I haven't seen you at Katsupari in such a long time," he said. "Will you come to visit me?" She promised she would, and they parted.

Next, Nancy found herself in a garden at the Katsupari Monastery. On a whim, she decided to attend a Satsang class led by Fubbi Quantz. She slipped into his classroom and took a seat against the back wall, liking the feel of being a student. Fubbi had just told the class about a visitor from the Soul Plane. When he finished his introduction for the guest speaker, he called Nancy to the front of the room. The topic he gave her was, "Why God's Love Is Worth Anything and Everything to Attain."

Her situation struck her as humorous. She realized how quickly ECK Masters set to work any chela who accepts their invitation to visit.

Looking at the sea of expectant faces in class, she began to talk. She spoke of all the suffering that a person may endure, but how trivial it is in comparison to the happiness, majesty, and splendor of God's love. This love is everywhere: in a child's hug, in a puppy's eagerness to play, and in the blooming of wildflowers on the lawn. The more we can accept divine love, the more we can receive. Yet, accepting God's love is only half of it. The other part is giving it back through service.

Then she asked the class, "What can you do to serve?" This led to a spirited discussion. Afterward, she asked them to pick a day, and at its onset to dedicate it to ECK. "See what happens."

This meeting with Fubbi Quantz was why she awoke so happy.

How can you find the elusive love of God? Follow the example of the three people in the stories above. Divine love comes through giving, and in no other way.

Divine love comes through giving, and in no other way.

7
LIVING DIVINE LOVE

Seeing.

Seeing, they see not; hearing, they hear not.

For only those with love do.

*Seeing, they
see not;
hearing, they
hear not.
For only those
with love do.*

*   *   *

*T*here is a poster by Oliphant Research that is an exercise in seeing. Taped up, it covers most of the top half of a door and is a confusing blur of gray lines, dots, and patterns all generated by a computer. It's like looking at a rough stone wall.

Someone instructs you to put your face against the chart and slowly draw back from it. Then this person asks what you see. The shapes have no pattern at all, but as you stare ahead, you can imagine an indistinct ⊕ symbol and some other vague shapes. But the instructor says, "That's not it. What else?" Try as you will, no other images reveal themselves from the mass of gray confusion.

Suddenly, a change comes over your vision. The poster appears to move, to come alive, and something is clearly taking shape right before your eyes.

Then the poster is alive. It's like a window into

another dimension, like a hologram. The flat, rough, gray wall turns into a granite wall of the ages into which a master engraver has set shapes like hearts, diamonds, mountains, and swirls. That is seeing the real image. When you tell the other person what you see, with excitement bubbling in your voice, the person nods.

"Yes, now you see the hidden images."

But there are two parts to this poster: the outer and inner dimensions. So far I've seen only the inner. Here, it looks as if an engraver hollowed out some objects deep within the stone wall. The outer side is still to come. Then, so I understand, hidden images appear to jump out from the wall to within inches of the observer. I've yet to see that part of the vision. Yet, based upon what I have already seen, I'm certain that this projecting image also exists, but I will have to make the effort to look at the poster correctly—in a wholly different way.

Persistence and the right frame of mind allows the viewer to penetrate the mystery of the computer-generated poster and see what is not easily apparent on the surface. Yet what about a crucial insight into the purpose of life? Who can see the multi-dimensional image of divine love?

Who can see the multi-dimensional image of divine love?

Many years ago, a teenage girl locked herself in the bathroom with the idea of ending her life with a bottle of sleeping pills. She took the pills and watched her face in the mirror. Her vision suddenly blurred. In the mirror she now saw the face of a man with blond hair and beautiful blue eyes, which were filled with tears. A single tear fell on his cheek. And with it, she sensed a mighty flow of love.

"No," he said, "it's not right to do this."

His appearance brought her to her senses. She

ran from the bathroom, told her parents about the sleeping pills, and they rushed her to the hospital in time. Years later, she recognized her guardian as the ECK Master Gopal Das. The mirror let her see into the world of love, a place unknown to her before. For had she known of it, there would certainly have been no reason to try to shorten her life. His love gave her the will to live. She thus learned about divine love.

It's often a surprise to people who for years have felt they know all about the love of ECK to find suddenly they have no idea what it is. How does this realization occur? It usually comes from a wholly unexpected quarter: a strong reaction to something the Mahanta, the Living ECK Master does. For example, most ECK initiates see the beauty of "Amazing HU," our version of "Amazing Grace." But not all do. What did John Newton compose when he wrote "Amazing Grace," if not a deeply touching love song to God? The words of the original song are all right for a Christian audience, but they needed spiritual tuning to fit the inner needs of ECKists. So I did that.

But in doing so, I pushed the buttons of some people who thought they knew the meaning of love but suddenly could not find it anywhere inside themselves. What happened? Maybe they never knew real divine love in the first place—or they simply forgot.

In closing, let me pass on to you a thought from a Higher Initiate whose own love for God recently met the test of faith.

"In contemplation," she writes, "I had asked to be shown something that I didn't know. I saw many mountains—each represented a different religion,

Years later, she recognized her guardian as the ECK Master Gopal Das. The mirror let her see into the world of love, a place unknown to her before.

Those who see and live divine love are of ECK.

art, occupation, way of life, etc. At the top of each mountain rose the few who were the lovers of life. Those who lived for consciousness, truth, beauty, and love. This, I was told, was the true brotherhood."

Those who see and live divine love are of ECK.

8
DO YOU FOLLOW LOVE OR POWER?

---

*E*arlier this month, an initiate of ECK took a hard look at the get-rich-quick consciousness of the eighties and the harm it does when ECKists pull schemes on their fellow initiates. He noted that the sidetrack for many chelas in the 1960s and 1970s seemed to be other paths, psychic phenomena, and the like. Today, it is not other paths but their own business dealings that chelas are trying to bring into the teachings of Eckankar. This get-rich-quick attitude is very persuasive.

He mentioned that there was support for a goal-oriented and success-oriented consciousness in *The Flute of God*. To quote from his letter: "Many times Paul seems to be explaining how to use the Universal Mind Power to manifest whatever we desire. I think there is a *great deal* of confusion about the fine line between the ECK power and the Universal Mind Power, not only on my part, but on the part of many others as well."

The writer is correct in his opinion. The simple thing I go back to repeatedly is this: Is our concern with the *power* or the *love* of ECK? People who overuse the word *power*, even in connection with the

The simple thing I go back to repeatedly is this: Is our concern with the power or the love of ECK?

35

ECK teachings, must be sure they really have the spirit of the path, and not the letter only.

This distinction is attested to by another initiate who is sensitive to the sharply differing behavior shown by those who follow love versus power. He observed that when two persons work over a desired thing, be it a material thing or a choice responsibility, often one will offer it freely to the other. Sadly, the other steps on the giver's face in an ungracious struggle for power. This bothered him, since he knew that the lessons of humility start with the offering. So often, while giving freely of something to another, he has gotten a lot of footprints in his face. With a wry sense of humor, he says he now knows that "the second part of this lesson of humility is that love, like the Mahanta, is faceless."

What are you but a spark of the Sugmad? Is your brother any less?

A number of chelas have been cheated by other chelas in the past few years. There is a certain amount of gullibility in people that grows in the face of getting rich quick, without any effort. There is an old saying: "You can't cheat an honest man." At the 1985 Creative Arts Festival in Anaheim, I spoke of the clean ethics needed when ECKists do business with each other. Shouldn't the same principles apply for business done with everyone? What are you but a spark of the Sugmad? Is your brother any less? Who is being fooled by acts of dishonesty—the Mahanta, you, the Law of Karma?

In that talk, I said that religions face the same problem among their members. Salt Lake City is sometimes referred to as a swindler's mecca. Oddly, most of the swindles are done by one member of the Mormon Church against another member. If an ECKist is cheated, and no other settlement can be reached, he is to go to the law-enforcement officers in his community and bring charges against the one who deceived him. Soul is in hostile territory as long as It resides in the worlds of the Kal Niranjan. The weak and immature in spirit are stepped on until, one day, they see that it's not necessary to be a rug for another's dirty shoes.

Business seminars run into the same problem. When speakers are invited to the better seminars, they are told that they are there to teach, not sell their own products. The same kind of self-discipline is needed among ECKists. If one's business would go bankrupt unless it were supported by other ECKists, it makes one wonder how sound the business really is. If an ECK initiate speaks at an ECK function or teaches a Satsang class, is he there to teach ECK or sell vitamins or property or the like?

A topic like this may seem unspiritual to some, but earth is the classroom of Soul. Daily experiences are closely intertwined with spiritual principles for those who have the higher spiritual insight. They can see that every experience is an opportunity for Soul to move toward the Light and Sound, or fall back.

The first writer noted that in many of the schemes, Mahdis (High Initiates) use the implied status of their rank in Eckankar to gain clients or participants in their businesses. When a Higher Initiate asked him to become involved in a vitamin company a number of years ago, he felt flattered. The same principle is operating today, and the writer called it "the awe of rank." Most chelas, when approached by a High Initiate for a business deal, tend to think, "Well, he's a Fifth Initiate, so it must be OK."

Earth is the classroom of Soul. Daily experiences are closely intertwined with spiritual principles for those who have the higher spiritual insight.

He also pointed to land deals as being detrimental to the integrity of Eckankar. He described one situation in which an ECKist was selling land at inflated prices to other initiates. The writer said of this, "The subtle misrepresentation of becoming a millionaire by simply buying some land is a real disservice to Eckankar. Although the land is not represented as being tied to Eckankar . . . the fact remains that he's using ECKists to obtain his goal."

As far as outer groups go, Eckankar is still young. These abuses will undoubtedly abound among our people as well as among those of organized religions. Look behind the thin curtain of deception, however. Is this not Soul facing Itself? It is unfortunate that some ECKists become willing channels for the Kal, but anyone who has the inner bond with the Mahanta will always find protection from these wolves. Others of us find the protection by following out the experience to its logical physical end: getting the help of legal officials to restore the stolen property. Cheating another person is certainly a blatant violation of his psychic space. The true initiate of ECK has his whole attention on the Sound and Light of God and would never do this sort of deed to another, who is really himself.

The true initiate of ECK has his whole attention on the Sound and Light of God and would never do this sort of deed to another, who is really himself.

The military is said to have a ruling to prevent such abuses in its community. A person of higher rank may not sell a product he is involved with to a person of lesser rank.

This is not to say ECKists are not to do business with each other. The point is to listen to the Inner Master for guidance in all the things we do, both on earth and in the inner worlds.

How you treat others tells everything about the spiritual condition of your heart.

Chapter Three

Self-Discipline

9

WHAT WE PREACH
AND WHAT WE PRACTICE

*N*ot so long ago, a teen came to a true, but sobering, conclusion about people in ECK. Some, she felt, would return to earth again. They would have to come back in spite of being Second, or even Fifth, Initiates.

What made her say this? She said they were not living the truths of ECK in their everyday lives, and it showed up in how they came to treat others. And how was that? From her observations, some people in ECK were still using power and control over others, as if such practices were their sole basis in ECK. This teen saw the gap between what some in ECK preach and what they practice. When a person's philosophy is so different from how he conducts himself with others, they are quick to notice. The only one not to see the discrepancy is the person himself.

Also of late, Canadian TV aired *The Last Dreamer*. It was a documentary on the beliefs of Sir Laurens Van der Post, an eighty-five-year-old aristocrat who years ago spent time with natives in Africa. He liked their simple ways. Perhaps it is unfair to make an assessment of his whole life

This teen said they were not living the truths of ECK in their everyday lives, and it showed up in how they came to treat others.

based solely upon a TV program, but it exposed the gaps between what he said and how he actually lived. He spoke of the ways in which people destroy the environment, while also hurting their inner selves, but not being aware of it.

Now, all this sounds very good. The host of the program then gave some background on Sir Laurens today. Van der Post claims to have a profound reverence for the natural world, but where does he live? In the bush in Africa? Perhaps he has a small cottage in England, far from the trampled path of civilization? Actually, he lives in the heart of London.

And with whom does this champion of the simple life and the environment spend his time? Does he seek the poor? Not at all. He circulates among the high society of Britain, and his circle of close friends includes Prince Charles. Yet, the narrator of the program fails to see the irony of this statement, which he made about Van der Post: "His heart and soul truly belong to Africa."

Such a gap between what a person preaches and what he does in his daily life is obvious to those beyond the net of the speaker's influence.

Of himself, Van der Post says that he is "a white bushman who never forgot the simple lessons of the desert." Somehow, there is a gap between British high society and the bushman, because each group lives a life completely alien to the other. The members of one group would feel quite out of place in the other.

Such a gap between what a person preaches and what he does in his daily life is obvious to those beyond the net of the speaker's influence. In fact, it is much like the alcoholic who chooses to do missionary work for God. Where does he go to do it? Why, directly to the bars and pubs to save the lost, and he has a drink or two while on his quiet mission. Who is he trying to fool?

So also is it in Eckankar when chelas act with self-righteousness toward others. This kind of behavior happens so often when a person is given a position of authority, and he then tries to control others. If someone has a suggestion, it is taken as a criticism and a personal attack, and the person who gave the idea in good faith finds himself at odds with a dictator. Don't say this doesn't happen in ECK. Unfortunately, it happens all too often with a few leaders who regard themselves as God's only true mouthpiece. To their minds, their own thoughts, words, and actions are pure; those of others are not.

So, is everyone who has taken the Second Initiation confirmed in bliss? Sadly, some will have to return. There is no blanket of protection for those who refuse to learn the lesson of divine love and humility. Can one abuse his position over another and expect Spirit to reward him for it?

Our belief about the liberation of Soul is unlike that of Christianity. A Christian may lead just about any kind of life he wants to, as long as he confesses his sins and accepts the atonement of Jesus in the final hour. In truth, the Law of God is not like that. It is much simpler. When we have love, we act with love. Love is the doorway to heaven. It is not power. It is not control. Nor is it anger. Unless love enters the heart, one has yet to find spiritual freedom.

When we have love, we act with love. Love is the doorway to heaven.

This is a very important Wisdom Note. How you treat others tells everything about the spiritual condition of your heart. Keep up with the Spiritual Exercises of ECK.

10
SPIRITUAL GRACE

This month I want to talk about moderation. Everything has a time and a place, like the four seasons. The renewal of spring, the abundance of summer, the harvest of autumn, and the time of rest provided to the land in winter all come in the right proportion. When given in balance, the seasons provide for a happy and abundant life.

If spring brings too much rain, floods destroy homes and property. Too little rain in summer causes drought. Frost too early in fall ruins the harvest. A winter too long and harsh wearies the spirit. Everything in the right amount brings an abundance of life and fulfillment.

Nature reflects the laws of ECK. Therefore, observe its workings in the habits of birds, the cycles of plants, and the instincts of the reptiles and mammals. All sing the glory of ECK; all teach the secrets of life. Watch the coming and going of clouds, the waxing and waning of the moon, and the rising and setting of the sun. They reveal the natural order of creation. Everything is right when there is neither too much nor too little for the time and

Nature reflects the laws of ECK. Therefore, observe its workings in the habits of birds, the cycles of plants, and the instincts of the reptiles and mammals. All sing the glory of ECK; all teach the secrets of life.

place. So is it also with your spiritual life.

Eat foods that are good for you, because they build and restore the temple where Soul resides. Accept your emotions. Permit your mind to study, explore, and grow. Give yourself time for rest and contemplation. Love God.

Go among the people of your community and see the Light of ECK in their eyes. Be awake among the sleeping. Therefore, love and show compassion, for joy comes from knowing your divinity. In children see men and women, for once they were so and shall be again. Give thanks for life, for it blesses you with revelations.

What more can ECK do than bring you love and understanding?

What more can ECK do than bring you love and understanding? Seasons come and go, youth turns to age, and familiar things change. Life gives and takes, but always gives again. Be thankful for wisdom, be grateful for existence.

In the next few years, the teachings of ECK will become more available to seekers. The Arahata needs a sense of generosity to give freely of the divine wisdom given to him or her. The ECK teacher's heart is open, willing to show others the way home to God. What room is there for jealousy among initiates? What can the ego offer Sugmad? Life is precious. Love it, and it will return unfoldment to you a thousand times. We live in a time of unequaled spiritual opportunity.

Our parents likely found the trials of their youth nearly unbearable. Today, as we look back on the problems of the thirties, forties, and fifties, they seem tame compared to the issues of pollution and overpopulation. The threat of hunger or the carnage of nuclear war were becoming very real to people then. Yet every global crisis came and somehow passed, and mankind still exists today. The troubles of each age are usually too much to bear, but humanity holds on to life despite everything.

This continuing unrest is a fact of world history. In ECK, we know that individual freedom will always be attacked by nations, rulers, and individuals that crave power. Does this frailty of mankind dampen our enthusiasm for living? Not in the least. We hold no illusions about the dark side of being, but we love life because of the spiritual potential it offers. Life is a jungle, but it is likewise a garden. It provides a time and place for unfoldment, because Soul is tempered by hardship. In spite of all, we look for ways to make things better for our loved ones, ourselves, and others. Life is for giving and loving, which fosters the nobility of spirit.

We hold no illusions about the dark side of being, but we love life because of the spiritual potential it offers.

This is my vision of what it means to be alive as the twentieth century is ready to greet the twenty-first. The ECK, or Holy Spirit, manifests little parts of Itself in the electronic and biologic technology of each age. Electricity is a manifestation of ECK, as is Soul. This world and the things in it are for exploration, study, and joy.

Immerse yourself in living. Pet a cat, hug a child, or love a dog. Eat an ice-cream cone, have some pie—but do all things in moderation.

My point is that ECKists do not have to shut themselves away from their families or communities. The daily struggles that life presents are opportunities to cultivate spiritual grace. God does not love you more if you stay inside all day to contemplate. Nor does God reserve a special place for you in heaven because you abstain from sweets. Moderation in all things is best. Ask yourself, What is for my highest good?

*Be aware of
the lofty needs
of Soul when
you choose a
habit, bever-
age, food,
thought, or
action. Your
mission in
this life is to
move to a
higher state of
being, to
become a
Co-worker
with God.*

This Wisdom Note is not a license for wanton living. Moderation is the key. Listen to the Mahanta in your dreams and in contemplation. He will guide you to the right foods and practices.

The ECK Masters teach that drinking alcohol and taking nonprescription drugs hinder spiritual advancement. Therefore they urge ECK initiates to let such habits go. These substances reduce an individual to the level of a brute and misdirect Soul's quest for God-Realization. Be aware of the lofty needs of Soul when you choose a habit, beverage, food, thought, or action. Your mission in this life is to move to a higher state of being, to become a Co-worker with God.

The ECK can only use a vessel according to its purity. Will water from a dirty cup quench thirst or bring disease? Look inside your cup.

Take a walk by yourself or with a loved one. Listen for the Voice of God in the sounds of nature. There is a plan to living; there is order. Love, and let God love you.

11
A PASSION FOR TRUTH

*I*n this Wisdom Note I want to go over some things with you about fear, group HU Chants, and Friday fasts.

We often get so into the enormity of living that we lose our sense of proportion and end up out of touch with reality. At the mercy of fear. The Sound Current is so vast and wonderful, but we hide in a corner of our world, crouching in terror. The Sound and Light of God can correct this affliction, but not if we are grounded in our little world. A Higher Initiate once reviewed the ups-and-downs of life and said, "What does it matter if everyone turns against you, so long as you have God?"

Sounds easy, doesn't it? Imagine yourself in a classroom with the Mahanta at a Temple of Golden Wisdom. You raise your hand and say, "I wouldn't be afraid of anything if you'd let me have one great experience with God." He replies, "Are you sure?" The Master's knowing smile gives you cause for reflection, because he knows how many people create a gulf between themselves and ECK. Ego makes this breach, in defense against truth. Until one's passion for truth outweighs his fear of himself, he

The Sound Current is so vast and wonderful, but we hide in a corner of our world, crouching in terror. The Sound and Light of God can correct this affliction, but not if we are grounded in our little world.

51

is stranded on the far side of life. Fear inhabits that place, while here, on this side, lives the Master's love. When love outshines fear, it transforms a chela into a complete spiritual being.

The changeover from ego to Soul, from fear to love, is done gradually, in such a way that an initiate can remain in control of himself. The Mahanta passes to him a gift of love, which is a burst of spiritual energy. This speeds the chela's unfoldment. He is able to accept more of the Light and Sound, and the truth contained in them. In this, he becomes a brighter light, bearing the message of the Living Word within him, to all who listen.

The Mahanta lets a new chela taste of the higher realization of Spirit during the First Initiation. There are two reasons for this: (1) the individual has earned the right, and (2) the Master wants to test his response to truth. In any case, the First Initiation begins to cancel a chela's karmic debt, which has created so much of the fear that dampens his zest for spiritual things.

A Higher Initiate, in Eckankar for over fifteen years, told of receiving the First Initiation six months after he began to study ECK. Lifted out of the body, he found himself in a cave on the Mental Plane. An opening led from the cave to a tunnel with blue-and-gold light swirling around inside it. In it, he heard the Music of ECK, a sound so entrancing that It pulled him into yet a higher world. He was now in a bright white area on the Soul Plane. The Light of God shone all around, filling him with overwhelming joy.

This area of the Soul Plane was without shape or form, and suddenly the chela was beset by fear. He was afraid of being in the Soul body, the infinite creation of Spirit. He felt totally alone. Finally, he understood what Peddar Zaskq (Paul Twitchell's spiritual name) meant when he spoke of Sugmad as the Great Alone. The chela knew he needed more spiritual training to survive in that lofty spiritual plane. He had first to master the Spiritual Exercises of ECK and fill himself with the purity of love. How can anyone stand before God without love?

In the end, the chela returned to the cave in the Soul body and there spotted his Mental body at rest. Overcome by panic, he tried desperately to crawl back into it. When he succeeded, he looked around to discover a group of Higher Initiates, who had watched his frantic struggle to reenter a bodily form. They were beside themselves with laughter. Recalling their own terror the first time they saw the infinite worlds of God, they said, "Now you know."

Yes, now he knew. But knowledge alone will not remove this fear. Today, fifteen and a half years later, he realizes that such anxiety is sparked by one's reluctance to accept his own divinity. This he calls "the fear of being Self." The Mahanta, knowing how little is gained by pushing someone where he is afraid to tread, has drafted certain spiritual exercises to aid him. They can help him reach his chosen place in heaven.

*   *   *

A word about chanting in groups: Sing the word HU. Recently, an Arahata was to lead a group and decided to have the initiates sing their own word silently. In the class discussion that followed, everything seemed to hover just on the edge of disruption. Through this experience, she recognized the power of the secret word. She now understands its

He had first to master the Spiritual Exercises of ECK and fill himself with the purity of love. How can anyone stand before God without love?

We want to grow spiritually strong, but not by risking good health. The mental fast is more beneficial for most people. Here are ways to do it.

use is solely for one's own contemplation. Even though her class chanted their secret words silently, it disturbed the group consciousness. HU, on the other hand, smooths it out.

Another point: The mental fast is more beneficial for most people than is the twenty-four-hour water fast. Here are ways to do it: Keep your thoughts upon the Mahanta all day long; throw your negative thoughts into a mental trash can; or ask, How would the Mahanta handle my problems today? One may also choose to do a partial fast of one meal on Friday, or a juice fast. Consult your family doctor before fasting to avoid possible injury, such as damage to muscles and connective tissue on long water fasts. We want to grow spiritually strong, but not by risking good health.

In closing, many ECK initiates use these Wisdom Notes and the *Mystic World* articles by the Living ECK Master in their Satsang or special group discussions. There is a reason they do that: They know these writings are to help them reach spiritual freedom in this present life.

12
AWE OF THE MIND

*G*od, freedom, and immortality have held man's interest since his first incarnation on earth. The ideal of something mightier than he was imprinted upon him as indelibly as the newborn calf is imprinted with the smells and sounds of its mother.

With the development of speech came the problem of putting the unspoken thoughts into words. Soon after came the rude development of primal philosophy. This began the play of the mind in things of the Spirit and was yet a boon for the elemental mind making the effort to reach beyond itself. But even philosophy became like an outgrown pair of shoes for the Soul that had unfolded to the limits of the Mental Plane and was prepared to go into the spiritual worlds of ECK.

The mind is an awesome tool. An optometrist told a patient that experiments had been done where lenses were made from prisms which inverted the image from the eye to the brain. The power of the mind was such that within a few days it rejected the topsy-turvy world, made a few adjustments, and turned the patient's vision upside up again.

God, freedom, and immortality have held man's interest since his first incarnation on earth.

As a further experiment, the doctor took the prism lenses from the patient. To everyone's surprise, the patient now saw the world inverted with the glasses off. The doctor had tricked the mind again, but the mind took immediate action to undo the trick. In a few days the patient's vision had returned to normal.

The newcomer to ECK is in the awkward position of giving up his awe of the mind, especially if he hopes to make any headway to God. Soul is therefore caught between the mind and the spiritual planes beyond it. Letting go of the mental apparatus is not easy to do, since all his training from youth on has been to put the powers of mental development on a sacred pedestal. The rigid world of the mind is actually a lock on the door of unfoldment that must first be seen for what it is, then removed with the help of a master locksmith, who is the Mahanta, the Living ECK Master. The Master knows firsthand what life is like with no freedom. But he is a graduate of the Mental world and knows the corridors that wind through the bureaucratic offices of the Kal.

Trouble itself is a gift from the ECK that forces us to learn Soul Travel and the spiritual laws that affect us and others.

The individual asks the Master questions he could get by himself, such as: "Can I be a member of a group other than Eckankar, while a student of the ECK discourses?" or "My health has turned bad; where can I get a healing?" The ECK gives the right answer to every question during the chela's spiritual exercises, if he will pay attention to the still small voice inside him. Trouble itself is a gift from the ECK that forces us to learn Soul Travel and the spiritual laws that affect us and others. The person beset by trouble is still the child of the ECK who is being allowed to grow into a fuller state of being.

But how often don't we curse the very trouble that is a blessing?

Thus, man is always in a position of trying to decide his relation with God. Is it God that causes ill things to occur, or is God simply too weak to stop whatever blemish there is in ITS nature that allows for the ill to exist at all?

Man squirms and slips in the mud of the Mental world as he looks for a solution to his quandary, but the key to his search for freedom and immortality is nowhere to be found in the Mental regions.

Good karma earns man the right to meet the Mahanta, but the likelihood is slight that the first meeting will produce any lasting impression upon the seeker, for the mind is running up an army of doubts that make him hesitate. He wonders if the teachings of ECK can really give him spiritual liberation. Since the mind is not of the stuff that can realize liberation, due to its mixed composition of Spirit and matter (and past experience lacks such a concept that it can use to make a comparison), the mind hands a rejection slip to the individual that reads: "Don't be fooled by ECK—there is no truth in It."

Heracleitus, the ancient Greek philosopher, had a mental concept of the ECK that reduced It to the level of the Mind Power. But Heracleitus saw that reality in the universe is at the mercy of the Law of Change, since things flow in the universe all the time. His famous observation in this regard was that a man cannot step into the same river twice. He identified the force that pervades the worlds as the *Logos*. Heracleitus did this five hundred years prior to the time Saint John put the term into his gospel. The ancient Greeks already knew that while

Man is always in a position of trying to decide his relation with God.

the Logos, the ECK, kept all the universes in order, It also pervaded the thoughts of sane and orderly men.

For us, the conflict of mind and Spirit boils down to a practical issue: Who takes care of things—God or me? Mostly, it is the initiate who must take care of himself. The Mahanta shows him how to get insights from the ECK through intuition, Soul Travel, or dreams. A person in the ECK line of unfoldment is soon able to get free of the hopeless human condition and rise above it into the pure states of wisdom, freedom, and immortality. But greater than these three attributes is the quality of love, which emanates from the God-Realized state.

How does one deal with life? The daily spiritual exercises must become a regular part of your regimen. Also, be of the mind to face trouble when it seeks you out; do not run from it.

But how does one deal with life, since the God State seems far too remote to even think about? The daily spiritual exercises must become a regular part of your regimen. Also, be of the mind to face trouble when it seeks you out; do not run from it. To face any problem, answer the five questions that follow: (1) What is really the problem that is upsetting me? (2) What most likely is the cause of it? (3) What solutions to deal with it come to mind? (4) Which is the one best solution? (5) How soon will I act upon the solution I have chosen?

Use these five points on the next problem that seems to be within your ability to handle. First, set small goals for yourself, and bigger ones later when your self-confidence is restored again. Above all, listen to the voice of the Mahanta to guide you through the trouble.

13
SPIRITUAL SHOWERS

The first thing I want to point out in this letter is the curious pattern of unusual weather that takes place before many ECK functions. Many of you in the advanced initiations already know that it is a reflection of the ongoing battle that goes on all the time between the ECK and Kal forces. The weather forecasters report snowstorms, tornadoes, and downpours that are out of season. The satellites are no help in the prediction of these events that leave the National Weather Service in a quandary as to an explanation for them.

The weather before a major ECK seminar turns tumultuous because the ECK lights up all the chelas around the world who have made plans to see the Mahanta, the Living ECK Master. The unruly weather conditions are the result of either of two things: (1) The immense Light and Sound of ECK from the chelas overpowers the ecology of the lower worlds, or (2) the Light and Sound in the ECKists is carried into the material worlds that have fallen into a recent state of darkness and negativity. Both these things, which are not the same at all, occur due to the wide separation that exists between the positive and negative poles.

The weather before a major ECK seminar turns tumultuous because the ECK lights up all the chelas around the world who have made plans to see the Mahanta, the Living ECK Master.

The higher one goes in the circles of ECK initiations, the more easily is he able to perceive the hidden causes in life.

The ability of one to discern the spiritual and material connection in events is due to the purification of the mind that is necessary before one can ever hope for the liberation of Soul. The higher one goes in the circles of ECK initiations, the more easily is he able to perceive the hidden causes in life. The ECKist develops a finely tuned balance between the four faculties of the mind, which are: the Chitta, the Manas, the Buddhi, and the Ahankar. The first two faculties gather impressions mainly through the perceptions of form, beauty, and taste, but they pass their initial findings on to the Buddhi for final judgment. The Buddhi, in a spiritual person, makes clean decisions and passes its judgments to the Ahankar for execution.

The ECKist holds a decided advantage over a man with a purely intellectual mind when it comes to running his everyday life. The intellectual has a problem in that he cannot easily make a clear-cut decision because the Buddhi faculty of his mind is misshapen. The function of decision making and discrimination in his mind is bent and weak, so that the Buddhi is overwhelmed by the pros and cons of an issue and can never make up its mind. The spiritual exercises drench the lower bodies with the Spiritual Current, creating an obvious mending in the mind to let it better carry out the orders of Soul.

The Spiritual Exercises of ECK take one then to either of two forms of contemplation: Samadhi or Nirvikalpa. Samadhi is really a much lower state than is Nirvikalpa, for it is only a psychic-world ability that enters the Mental Plane. In Samadhi, one becomes one with the Kal, although the enlightened one in cosmic consciousness generally feels he has gotten the highest realization of God. The first stages of Samadhi come when the chela meets the Mahanta outside the physical body. The Mahanta meets him here and gives the First Initiation, and thereafter Samadhi becomes the tool for Soul to escape the worlds of death in the worlds below Sat Lok.

Nirvikalpa is the higher form of Samadhi that begins on the Fifth Plane, where the seeker cannot tell himself apart from the ECK. It is an upper-world form of contemplation that spans from the ECKshar to the God Consciousness, which is finally attained by the Kevalshar. Here the objective life is shut out and one is beyond the state of total awareness, which occurs in the Hukikat Lok; he is in the kingdom of heaven. It is good for you to have a road map to identify the place reached during contemplation.

The initial state of God-Realization thus begins to drift into the universe of the individual after the Eighth Initiation. At the Ninth Plane, truth becomes still more apparent as he enters into the first degree of the Vairagi Order. A higher portion of truth comes at the Tenth Plane, where one enters into the divine wisdom pool. Beyond the Tenth Plane, the Kevalshar, the initiate of the Eleventh Circle, learns that love is truth and truth is love, and that all is ECK. For without love there cannot be truth. But this is the higher love, not the personal one that takes note of a person's own wishes instead of the good of all.

Without love there cannot be truth. But this is the higher love, not the personal one that takes note of a person's own wishes instead of the good of all.

Truth becomes more sublime for an individual who develops in himself the capacity to give more compassion and love to all creatures. The Mahanta, the Living ECK Master is the spiritual head of the Vairagi Order of ECK Adepts, but the wisdom and compassion of senior members of the Order surpass even his ability. Such is the way of the Sugmad, to assign certain spiritual duties to the new spiritual leader of ECK. The ageless Adepts keep on with their service to life in perfect accord with the over-all direction of the hierarchy, for which the Mahanta is the director during his term of office.

I am always happy to get letters from those of you in the First Initiation who have a recognition of your meeting with the Nuri Sarup, the Light body, of the Mahanta.

14
THE DISCIPLINE OF LOVE

---

his letter is a little bit about everything. First of all, a comment about the HU Chant and its place in our spiritual life. At the 1987 European and African ECK seminars we sang HU in a different fashion than usual. Instead of singing the clear, simple HU in an unadorned manner, we sang it while repeating in our minds, "What is the HU?"

Singing HU in this way has its place, but it is not to replace the time-honored chant used in our group HU Chants for years.

The HU Chant we all know is clean—uncluttered by any mental baggage. It is Soul's song of love to God, the Sugmad. The second way of chanting, which is done while silently repeating, "What is the HU?" has another purpose. It can often break through the rigid mind patterns of one who is having no experiences of Sound or Light. It helps him fix his attention upon the word HU to find its greater significance.

The HU Chant just mentioned did give an ECK initiate who attended the 1987 ECKANKAR European Seminar an experience with Sat Nam, the

The HU Chant we all know is clean—uncluttered by any mental baggage. It is Soul's song of love to God, the Sugmad.

ruler of the Soul Plane. She had been listening to the Living ECK Master's talk on Saturday night. While listening, she reflected upon the number of times the Law of Gratitude had cropped up in other talks and workshops during the day. Now, when the Living ECK Master introduced the HU Chant, she shut her eyes and chanted with the audience, silently asking three times, "What is the HU?"

She reopened her eyes a moment to look at the Master. Then closing her eyes again, she saw in her Spiritual Eye a shining face with a bald head: Sat Nam.

He said, "The Mahanta has taught you the HU to reach me." Seeing him like this also gave her something to be grateful for.

HU is indeed a powerful word to chant for spiritual upliftment.

HU is indeed a powerful word to chant for spiritual upliftment. *The Shariyat* says of it: "In this mantric sound all the positive and forward-pressing forces of the human, which are trying to blow up its limitations and burst the fetters of ignorance, are united and concentrated on the ECK, like an arrow point."

The HU Chant in which the individual repeats "What is the HU?" to himself is a Mental Plane exercise. It is best not to sing it at group HU Chants because when attention is put on the mind, it can cut off the ECK flow for some initiates. This version of the HU chant is to be used sparingly, in private: when it seems to be one's only recourse in reaching a new understanding of HU. The regular HU chant is to be sung at ECK gatherings.

Now I'd like to repeat a point made elsewhere about unfoldment. Every now and then chelas who left ECK years ago write to ask if they may continue their studies at the same initiation level as when they left. These people don't realize that when they go inactive, their spiritual unfoldment comes to a halt—and then begins to go in reverse. Why is that?

The ECK Life Stream is forever expanding and moving forward. So when a person takes a rest from active study, the other ECK initiates keep moving on. Soon he is left far to the rear. If he stays away too long, he may have to resume the path at a lower initiation. It may surprise a Fifth Initiate to find that after several years of absence from discourse study, he has slipped back to the Fourth level. When ready to move forward again, that is the place from which he must continue his study of ECK.

Going in another direction for a moment, I would like to speak about the discipline of love. Any experience a person gets, whether here or in the other worlds, adds to the sum of what he is, knows, and perceives.

For example, a camera is a camera. Yet put it in the hands of two different people, and the result is two different grades of pictures. One photographer may be a world-class portrait photographer, while the other is your average birthday-party-snapshot historian. What accounts for the variation in the quality of the photos, since the camera is the same?

It is discipline—the discipline of love. The quality depends upon each person's inner development. Put another way, it shows how much more disciplined love the one can put into a photo than the other can. Any great achievement is always powered by disciplined love. A great person has discipline in the field of his expertise, and this is where he lets his great love shine.

Let's bring this down to your everyday life. If

Any great achievement is always powered by disciplined love.

loneliness is a problem but you are mobile, join activities in your community. You can be a silent channel for ECK while at the same time balancing your outer and inner life.

One initiate is taking a night course in art appreciation. She sees it as a great opportunity for learning and expects to have a good time doing it. Here also is the discipline of love. We can combat loneliness by doing new things, things we may enjoy. It gets us out among people where we can watch the ECK manifest through our new experiences. This lets us emerge from our shells in a quiet way.

The discipline of love means doing something to overcome harmful states like loneliness, and thus we become a greater channel for God.

The discipline of love means doing something to overcome harmful states like loneliness, and thus we become a greater channel for God.

A RESA, contemplating upon what stood between her and Mastership, received this from the Mahanta: "When your heart is so open to the love for God that your every action, word, thought, and feeling manifests the pureness of the Light and Sound of God, then you will know that you have achieved Mastership."

The creative techniques, the Spiritual Exercises of ECK, are the key that guides wandering Soul to the inner temple.

CHAPTER FOUR

Keys to Inner Worlds

15
HOW TO OPEN THE DOOR INSIDE YOU

*T*he true follower of ECK is careful with the terms he uses to describe contemplation or the creative techniques. Correctly, they are called the Spiritual Exercises of ECK, rather than meditation. He knows that there is a vast difference between them.

In ECK, the initiate goes inward and does something. Chanting the secret word imparted to him during the initiation, he contemplates on the Sound and Light, and the form of the Living ECK Master. Upon meeting the Inner Master, the initiate is taken to the inner temple and there partakes of the Audible Life Stream of ECK.

Meditation differs in that it takes the passive approach to the secret worlds. It is interesting to note that the spiritual lethargy and poverty of India reflect centuries of meditation. The yogi goes inward to still the mind. His goal is to attain bliss and joy and become one with God, unaware that union with God is not possible. It is within the destiny of Soul, however, to become a Co-worker with the Sugmad and enter into the true realm of heaven.

In ECK, the initiate goes inward and does something.

71

Each profession demands a course of study, and success follows by doing homework. The same is true in ECK.

Hardly everyone is qualified to pass through the door into the inner worlds when he first comes into Eckankar. He must first dedicate some time to the spiritual exercises in order to build up spiritual stamina. Who would expect to become a pilot, doctor, lawyer, nurse, engineer, secretary, or teacher without the self-discipline of a thorough training program? Each profession demands a course of study, and success follows by doing homework. The same is true in ECK.

At a HU Chant one evening, an individual heard the Sound come in this way: "Very soon after we started to chant HU, a strange sound like a wind was heard, and then I heard above the HU the flute playing with the rich, dark-colored sound. At first, I thought it came from some source on the outer, but I realized very soon that it came from within."

The spiritual exercises given in the ECK discourses are secret, intended for the initiate who has earned the right to practice them. The whole key to the secret worlds lies in the initiate's personal word and his creative use of it. Nevertheless, the word is powerless until the Mahanta imbues it with life during the sacred initiation.

Furthermore, the Mahanta, the Living ECK Master lays out a series of spiritual exercises that lead to the inner temple. It is like the woodsman who leads a traveler through the dense forest in order to find sanctuary in a secluded cabin that offers food and shelter. The journey of Soul through the negative worlds leads Soul to Jivan Mukti, the liberation from the Wheel of Reincarnation that is attained during the initiation of the Fifth Circle.

An ECKist found that "since I learned of Eckankar, strange and wonderful things are happening to me. I feel as though I am becoming the center of my universe, the hub of my wheel of life here on this physical plane." That ECKist is mastering the self-discipline required for progress on the path to God.

The following illustrates the relationship between the Master and the initiate. A self-taught Sunday artist devoted years to developing her skill as a painter. She had spurned art lessons, believing them a limit to her natural talent. Finally, she was persuaded to enroll in an art class at a community college. The teacher, she noticed, had carefully distilled techniques from successful artists and imparted them to the students. Instead of limitations, the woman found freedom to blend these deft touches into her own work and greatly enhance the quality of her paintings. This is also how the ECK enriches the life of the initiate.

The ECKist absorbs the secrets of life through the creative techniques compiled by the Order of the Vairagi Masters. They are connected with the ECK and bring about a gradual change of attitude in the individual that is only for his benefit.

Every Living ECK Master struggles to put into words the inexpressible truth of ECK. All the Master can do is to point the way and give encouragement to the chela in his own efforts to find the revelation of God. The creative techniques, the Spiritual Exercises of ECK, are the key that guides wandering Soul to the inner temple.

The creative techniques, the Spiritual Exercises of ECK, are the key that guides wandering Soul to the inner temple.

16
OUTER ANSWERS TO INNER QUESTIONS

For every question that comes up about ECK and how It works in one's daily life, there is an answer to satisfy the mind in a past Wisdom Note.

Frequently the Inner Master answers while the question is still being put to paper in the monthly initiate report. An ECKist grappling with a spiritual question recently reported: "Interesting tidbit—you know how it is that the Wisdom Notes answer the questions that are in the minds of the chelas? Well, I started rereading the Wisdom Notes recently and, sure enough, there was my answer."

Soul must walk Its own path to God. It alone undertakes the spiritual preparation necessary to reach God Consciousness. The Living ECK Master guides and assists the individual until the goal is won. The chela must always stand on his own two feet, depending solely upon inner guidance.

The questions that bother us will be answered. When we reach into the heart of God, the Master releases us so he can work with another who is struggling to gain his place in the spiritual worlds.

Soul must walk Its own path to God. It alone undertakes the spiritual preparation necessary to reach God Consciousness.

Regularly I get letters from ECKists who tell of a lack of success with the Spiritual Exercises of ECK. There is an absence of visual, audible, or out-of-body experiences, and they feel they face failure in their spiritual quest. This is not so. There are many facets to the path of Eckankar, and Soul chooses the ones that fit It. When the pink initiation slip arrives in the mail, that is enough indication that one has earned the right to move into the next higher circle of initiation. The decision is ours. No one else can tell us if we are ready for more of the Sound and Light of ECK.

The secret teachings are given a little at a time. The path of ECK is to enhance one's own efforts toward God-Realization. The curtain will be opened for the memory of the inner experiences when Spirit sees we are ready. This protection is afforded by the Living ECK Master so that the individual maintains a balance in his everyday life.

The path of ECK is to enhance one's own efforts toward God-Realization.

The expansion of consciousness comes subtly. A woman reported a problem for which she desired an answer. Not able to get it clearly, she asked Spirit for help in the dream state. She said, "I want it clear, so I will know exactly what I am supposed to do. I want it in black-and-white! If it has to be written on the blackboard." The dream state had previously given her the answer through symbols which she was not able to interpret. Upon awakening the next morning she felt the ECK had not given her a reply. Nevertheless, that evening she opened the newspaper and staring in her face was the answer. She recognized the subtle working of ECK and is more aware of the answers that show up in the most unusual places. In conclusion, she said, "Where could I get something more in black-and-white than in the newspaper?"

One uses patience with the spiritual exercises but, more importantly, fills one's heart with love when going to the inner temple. A woman from the Midwest felt a lack of success with the spiritual exercises. It dawned on her that she was being too mechanical and trying too hard. "I wasn't putting any love into it," she writes, "just repeating words. I couldn't focus my attention anywhere. I still don't see a Light, but I sing the word with all the love I have. I can feel all that love and so much more returning to me."

A number of you have recognized that working for the ECK is a most important part of the spiritual life. Through our efforts the message of God is carried to all corners of the community. Further, we can do a charitable deed for another in the name of the Mahanta which gives the protection of the karmaless act.

It is important to chant one's word at home, on the job, in the Satsang. It leads Soul to the inner temple where It finds Spirit and liberation from the Kal.

One uses patience with the spiritual exercises but, more importantly, fills one's heart with love when going to the inner temple.

17
RIGHT ACTION

*R*ichard Baxter was a writer and a member of the Puritan clergy in seventeenth-century England. He had a motto that you can still profit from as an ECKist today: "In necessary things, unity; in doubtful things, liberty; in all things, charity."

First, unity in and with ECK makes you a tower of strength. To be strong, you need this closeness with the Holy Spirit in all three basic areas of life—within yourself, with your family, and with the world. Unity in ECK means strength. Second, in doubtful things give liberty. Liberty here means to take a chance on yourself and others. If you think of a better way to serve life, a way no one else has thought of yet, take the liberty of doing it. Liberty is like a lot of other spiritual gifts: use it or lose it. Third, in all things give charity. This means to be generous with yourself, with those who are close, and with as many others as you can.

Baxter's three points are important, for they show how to enter the spiritual community of ECK. In each case, notice that to live in the fullest expression of life, you must always give of yourself to the

To be strong, you need this closeness with the Holy Spirit in all three basic areas of life—within yourself, with your family, and with the world.

people in the world around you. And what of your needs? Of course, you also take care of them—for that is the middle way of balance—but the ECK will help you.

So to have unity, support it; to have liberty, use it; and to have charity, show it.

That brings up you and your quest for spiritual realization in ECK today. John Truby is a teacher who holds classes in story structure, and he shows his students how to use that knowledge to write better stories. Yet he does more than just teach stories: He teaches the laws of life. He shows that the aim of life is to reach a higher state of realization, a goal that is anything but easy to achieve.

In his tapes, *World Myth: Writing the New Stories*, Truby speaks of the need for a person to become an adult. This is a clear parallel to the works of ECK, in which an individual has the desire to become an adult in the worlds of God: a mature spiritual being. Truby calls it "the search for understanding the self." But we look for a state beyond this understanding of self and grasp for the highest state of all—Co-worker with God. Truby, in his class on myth, says that many subtle inner changes need to occur before you can reach the ideal state. But human nature is so slow to move to a higher level that any change often goes unnoticed.

A person who wishes to move from the ego to the higher self in understanding does so through right action.

He, like us, recognizes both the ego and the Higher Self (Soul). A person who wishes to move from the ego to the higher self in understanding does so through right action. We call it *dharma*. Truby is very careful to point out that such right action has nothing to do with good and evil, nor has it anything in common with sin, the narrow moral structure of Christian belief.

Right action means something more. It means that you must figure out the natural, or universal, order of things and act in harmony with it.

Yet how many initiates of ECK know how to live a life of right action? What keeps you from living it? Truby is a good student of human nature, and he finds that the human flaw that keeps people from understanding the self is pride. It is our old friend, the offspring of vanity—one of the five passions. Pride upends more people from the seat of Soul than just about anything else. Pride shows itself in a love for titles, a need to look good to your peers, and the act of comparing the lesser abilities of others to your own. Pride is an expression of ego, says Truby. It keeps you from seeing your higher self and from taking right action.

So all this comes back to charity. Until you begin to practice the charity that you expect from others, you will go nowhere on the spiritual path. Once you make room for charity, it will make room for you. Only then will you have the community—and unity—of Spirit within you, with your family, and with others in the world.

In California and elsewhere, ECK chelas are beginning to work more toward having such a community of Spirit. They want to know each other as people with jobs, hobbies, and families—not only in their roles as ECK leaders. Ask the Mahanta to help you change inside. Once this happens, you will feel a natural bond with others, especially those of the ECK community. You will begin to treat them as spiritual equals.

All this is right action. It is inseparable from unity with Spirit, liberty, and charity.

Until you begin to practice the charity that you expect from others, you will go nowhere on the spiritual path.

18

AN AWAKENED CONSCIOUSNESS

At the Temple of Askleposis on the Astral Plane, chelas asked the Mahanta for the secret of manifold creation and were told of the individualized units of consciousness (Souls). Each Soul was positioned in random space, in an order of a kind, but was still in the unawakened state.

For the Sugmad to realize Itself, the individualized units began to be grouped according to like qualities. First, small clusters of like were formed. These then merged with other groups under a larger umbrella of like qualities. This grouping of smaller units into ever larger ones of increasing qualities of likeness made for the instant alignment of units from one end of creation to the other. All the units were in communication with units near them, which were there due to closest similarity. In the end, the ECK was one. All the individual Souls, while retaining their uniqueness, were aligned with their beingness toward the Sugmad. In this way does the Sugmad realize Itself in manifold creation.

The living link between the macrocosm, the Sugmad, and the individual Soul (the microcosm) is the ECK. Any record of this relationship is the

At the Temple of Askleposis on the Astral Plane, chelas asked the Mahanta for the secret of manifold creation and were told of the individualized units of consciousness (Souls).

83

Shariyat-Ki-Sugmad. The Shariyat is a highly organized system of information, knowledge, and wisdom. Its truth is not put together from haphazard pieces of experience, but it is as orderly as a city whose well-planned streets are marked by easy-to-see street signs.

An individual may follow his interests into the area of high wisdom, which is like the mansions of the rich. Each mansion on every street has a story to tell. Another individual may be attracted by a practical, causal outpouring of the Shariyat. He would be like a businessman who makes a visit to the business district of a city. He goes into its hotels, restaurants, stores, and shops. Each place of business has its own story to tell, and there are many stories.

The writer who chronicles the Shariyat is like a reporter who walks the streets of a city in search of a story. He stops where he will to report on what he sees. Only a small part of the whole Shariyat can be, or ever has been, put into the printed word. Most of it comes straight into the individual during the Spiritual Exercises of ECK as the Living Word, the Sound and Light of ECK. Every article or Wisdom Note by the Mahanta, the Living ECK Master is taken from the Shariyat that is in some inner city.

There are twelve or more volumes of the Shariyat that pertain to the experiences of Soul as It makes Its way home to God. Its words are fitted to the needs and understanding of the times. Since the holy scripture is written around the experiences of Soul, its words are truth.

During the immature portion of Its existence in the worlds of matter, Soul knows only to serve Itself. As life rubs its lessons into Soul, there is a loss of

Every article or Wisdom Note by the Mahanta, the Living ECK Master is taken from the Shariyat that is in some inner city.

attachment to the things of the world. Soul moves into the higher states of consciousness, and as It does, there is no desire so great as the one to humbly give service to the Sugmad.

Soul becomes the Knower by doing. The spiritual life is the active life, where fears are put aside by the love for new vistas. The pain of living does not grow less as the individual expands into the more refined levels of consciousness, but, indeed, it may grow greater because his sensitivities are finer. The ECK initiate is the leader among people in regard to spiritual things, and there is no disputing the Light and knowledge that is carried within him.

An initiate told of her experience at the recent death of her father. She had received a call to see him and found him on his deathbed at home. As the old man's translation grew closer, the rest of the family, none of them chelas, did not want to go into his room. The daughter wondered why he should be alone in this, his finest hour. She and her husband went into the room. She knelt by the bed, rubbed her father's hand and head, and just talked to him.

The Inner Master was telling her what to say. She asked her father if he would like to be with a daughter who had died in infancy, to which he nodded yes. "Then go to her," she said. "Go to the others and go to the Light." Just before this he had been having trouble with the death process but now translated peacefully.

The initiate made the comment that "Frankly, death is no more than what we do in our spiritual exercises . . . one just does not come back to the physical. Sad? I cannot be; it was such a beautiful experience. It makes no sense to be afraid."

Her mother's minister was also in the home

Soul becomes the Knower by doing. The spiritual life is the active life, where fears are put aside by the love for new vistas.

then, but he did not seem to know what to do. He introduced himself to the father but appeared uncomfortable, and was glad when the daughter took over. The ECK initiate was more ready to help the dying man than was the ordained minister. The Mahanta gives us help in countless ways to face the troubled times.

The Mahanta gives us help in countless ways to face the troubled times.

"The wretched, the poor, the unhappy, and those who are in need are drawn unto the Mahanta," reads *The Shariyat*, Book One, "for those who are poor in heart are the greatest recipients of his love."

These are the ones who come to the Mahanta with no complaints, but with gratitude and love. The confusion of the mind has brought them a life of anguish, of not being able to make a clear decision on things material or spiritual. But having found the Mahanta, they will never leave him.

They are the awakened individualized units of consciousness that have heard the Music of God. No earthly desire can ever keep them from seeking the spiritual mountain, for it is they who see and accept the gift of love that he gives them for their recognition of it.

The circle has come full from the macrocosm to the microcosm, and back again. See and know the meaning in it for you.

When the ECK heals us, It first turns our lives over like a gardener turning shovelfuls of dirt in the garden.

CHAPTER FIVE

Spiritual Healing

19
GIFTS OF HEALING

*I*t's been a very good year. The Year of Spiritual Healing began on October 22, 1985, and its force will continue into the foreseeable future, blending smoothly into the Year of the Arahata, which began on October 22, 1986. Each year melts into the next, and the power of each is added to future years.

The Year of Spiritual Healing brought a number of healings to the initiates of ECK, although many of these changes will only begin to manifest in the months to come. Spiritual healing goes to the root of a problem, and it is inevitable that a whole new foundation is built for the chela. Here in Minnesota, for example, the urgency of construction workers trying to beat the first snowfall is something to see. A marshy tract of land is to be cleared and a business complex constructed upon it before the cold weather makes construction impossible. Huge land-moving equipment dredged out the marshy land, and other machines put down layer upon layer of soil over the soft ground. The dirt is packed down, the ground water drained away, and slowly the parcel of property is being brought above the flood level of a nearby river.

Spiritual healing goes to the root of a problem, and it is inevitable that a whole new foundation is built for the chela.

91

The Mahanta, the Living ECK Master has done the same kind of careful groundwork in the body of ECK chelas during the Year of Spiritual Healing. The whole process of spiritual rejuvenation seems ponderously slow, but the chela is being conditioned for strength. His indecisiveness is being taken away and replaced by sound direction. The healings will be physical, emotional, mental, and spiritual. These will manifest for some time. This means the effects of the Year of Spiritual Healing will continue into the months to come.

A Higher Initiate wrote of chelas in his area who began to cooperate with each other for the first time in 1986. Tongue in cheek, the letter writer said this was indeed a miracle. The emotional body of the ECK chelas has undergone spiritual healing. The healing has brought a harmony which now allows the setting up of the RESA program. The contentions in some regions of the world that prohibited the spreading of the ECK message are greatly reduced. The healing has brought an awareness to many that the reason for our existence is indeed much greater than to spend all our time in fights with each other. The message of ECK is too important to be left in the care of irresponsible individuals who want only to fight each other. The spiritual healing has opened their eyes to the need for reaching people with the news of spiritual liberation.

Enter the Year of the Arahata, the year of the teacher. In 1986–87, the objective is to develop programs to carry the writings of ECK everywhere. I'm asking each RESA to sponsor at least one or two ECK regional seminars this coming year. This program will be uniform throughout the world. Two sample programs for the seminars were recently released through the Spiritual Services department at the 1986 World Wide of ECK. In this new year, we will begin to move quietly into the public stream again with ECK. Many of you are well qualified to teach an ECK class and will find the experience an enjoyable one. The new people who are approaching ECK may look at It differently from what you did. Be sensitive to their needs, respond to their questions, but keep before them the desired goal of Self- and God-Realization. But understand that this early in their studies, they may be more interested in other phases of Eckankar.

When the ECK heals us, It first turns our lives over like a gardener turning shovelfuls of dirt in the garden. The earth must be made fresh before it can grow anything. Although a good number of individuals have received a spiritual healing this year, many of them are unaware of it. Some of them even blame the Master for the mountains of trouble in their lives. Don't they realize that the Master takes the raw material of healing from their own karma, and from this dust the spiritual giant is raised? And so the Mahanta stands back, says nothing, and lets them go their ways. Eventually, they will see the blessings that have come to them, although they may still be unwilling to attribute it to the intervention of the Mahanta. But how can anything worthwhile happen to an ECK initiate unless it be through the Mahanta? This they fail to see.

It is the ECK that brings changes. The whole pattern of your life already lies unmanifested before you. All that remains for something spiritual and good to happen is your agreement that this is the right time for it. This agreement is made by

It is the ECK that brings changes. The whole pattern of your life already lies unmanifested before you. All that remains for something spiritual and good to happen is your agreement that this is the right time for it.

Soul, however, and the individual in the physical consciousness is usually unaware of the pact made with Spirit. Then when the tests begin, and the changes come, he chafes at them. Inflamed by his emotions, he blames others for the turbulence that suddenly appears. In reality, it is brought about by his own resistance to the Holy Spirit.

When an individual begins a certain service to the ECK, he may beg the Master to tell him immediately when he is slipping from grace. But when the time comes and he needs a word of admonition, he cannot hear the warnings. He is told in many different ways, at a number of different levels of consciousness, but who can talk to pride? This leaves the Master no alternative but to stand aside and wait until life can teach the individual better.

The Mahanta does not glory in the troubles of others. When he sees them shutting off the Holy Spirit, he feels a genuine sadness. His love for them is greater than they know. When they cry, he cries with them; when they laugh, he laughs too. But there is little to laugh about when they become insensitive to the Sound and Light. This is when the Master weeps the most, and they don't know it.

Keep your heart clean before Sugmad and all will be well with you in this new year of ECK.

Who can talk to pride? This leaves the Master no alternative but to stand aside and wait until life can teach the individual better.

20
LETTING THE
ECK HEAL YOU

The ECK Satsang classes are the mainspring of the outer works in ECK. At one time in the past, Arahatas ended class with a fifteen-minute contemplation, which was followed by a brief discussion. This was a monthly spiritual laboratory to help chelas contact the nondimensional consciousness, the ECK.

Some time back, during a Satsang contemplation, two chelas shared the same inner experience. Each had gone to a Golden Wisdom Temple and had seen an enormous old book that was the Shariyat-Ki-Sugmad, the Way of the Eternal. Both were fully aware of each other's presence in this temple. In a corner of the room stood a water pitcher, from which flowed a beautiful blue water—the outpouring of the Holy ECK. Their mutual visit was proof to them that the Golden Temple was more than a product of the imagination.

The discussion at the end of contemplation explained to another chela how to recognize her own real experiences in ECK. Her complaint was that she had no recall of the inner revelations. She had seen but a tiny point of white light; still, the

The ECK Satsang classes are the mainspring of the outer works in ECK.

light was expanding in each contemplative session. It was a sign of expanding consciousness, for her Spiritual Eye was being opened to the light of the other worlds. To her, the light was an all-too-familiar companion, so much so that it had meant nothing to her. But from that Satsang on she was a new creature. Her subjective side began to flourish, and she developed a clear, inner sight into the things of the invisible sphere about her.

Frankly, the human race is up against a crisis as compelling as that which ECK Master Fubbi Quantz faced before the discovery of America. The practice of the Spiritual Exercises of ECK is about the only solution to meet it.

Frankly, the human race is up against a crisis as compelling as that which ECK Master Fubbi Quantz faced before the discovery of America. The practice of the Spiritual Exercises of ECK is about the only solution to meet it. The problem in the late fifteenth century was that the nutrition of the European people was in a shocking state. The people had little energy left over after the day's work for contemplation, the moment of quiet which is the sweet drink of Soul. Fubbi Quantz thus set into motion the events that led Columbus to sail his three tiny ships westward into unknown waters for the discovery of the Americas, where abundant food could be gotten to revive the food stock of the Old World.

The challenge today is to go beyond modern medicine in a search for effective treatments of illness. Statistics well prove that the life span of people is growing longer, but a serious gap still exists between the healing of common ills and a knowledge of their primary cause.

This concern strikes some as being far afield of the spiritual works, but is not *all* life the spiritual life? The Shariyat recognizes man's compulsion to create a plethora of products for the marketplace, but many of the goods are neither wanted nor needed by the public.

In a talk with Paul Twitchell, Fubbi Quantz listed five things one could do to work out his destiny in ECK. The chela should be working on (1) "spiritual unfoldment," (2) "the curing of man's ills," (3) "delving into the secrets of life," (4) "plumbing the ocean's depths," and (5) "reaching out to the world of God through Soul Travel."

A great deal of this is starting to come about in the four service orders. Chemists, physicists, doctors, homeopaths, and others are uniting forces in ECK for research into healing. This silent work is a sorely needed contribution if man is to survive the serious pollution of thought, air, soil, and water. In the future, states, provinces, or countries will have annual summertime retreats, or campouts, for the purpose of holding informal gatherings to see what common bonds of interest can be turned to a good use in society.

The Ancient One comes in every age to redeem Soul from the ravages of materialism. He is the Mahanta, the Living ECK Master, who teaches survival on every level, from the Anami Lok right down to earth. The creative arts include other disciplines besides art, music, or painting. Skills such as writing, teaching, parenting, and business, among a host of others, are being added to coming ECK seminar workshops.

We want to be as self-reliant as possible, and karma will waste away without the added burden on us from false concepts embedded by previous religious paths that poverty merits some special status in heaven. The Sugmad cares little if coins fill our pocket, but Soul is to master spiritual survival on all planes. It is then ready for service in Its cause.

The Mahanta, the Living ECK Master teaches survival on every level, from the Anami Lok right down to earth.

When someone pours out his troubles to you, remember to declare yourself a vehicle for the Sugmad, the ECK, and the Mahanta. Be there as a channel for the ECK which does the actual healing.

The silent listeners are the instruments of the Mahanta who give solace to mankind. When someone pours out his troubles to you, remember to declare yourself a vehicle for the Sugmad, the ECK, and the Mahanta. Create a mood of stillness where the troubled one may sense the presence of the divine power, and be there as a channel for the ECK which does the actual healing. Then watch the heart in mending. Midway through the conversation the individual will have some kind of a sympathetic response, and it is at this point that he has opened his heart to the Spirit of Love. This is like the turn of a golden key. He may weep, or suddenly exclaim, "I now know what to do." Note this change in him but continue with the meeting for several more minutes so that he can gather in the gift of Spirit, and let his heart heal over. Oftentimes, he is not mindful that the ECK has slipped into his core like a golden dove, to put his troubles to rest. The changes from Divine Spirit burn deep, and they begin to work for his benefit in the days and weeks to come.

This is a preview and a signpost for future Co-workers with God. Love one another, therefore, in the purity of your hearts.

21
LIFE IS SIMPLY CHANGE

The password in ECK is change, for all living things are in flux, moving toward growth or decline. Movement into unknown conditions brings stress, and this can end in dis-ease.

In today's fast society, time chases us to work, to the doctor and dentist, to recreation, even to and from meals. Time did not always have this grip upon people. Before Edison's bulb turned night into day, the craftsman awoke with the animals and worked as long as natural light would let him. The pace of life was slower, because karma was slower.

But with the emergence of the spring-driven clock in the fifteenth century, time seemed to speed up. The day finally came to be divided into arbitrary parts, into hours and minutes. New stress has come into play with mankind's ability to keep good track of time. Employees are fined if tardy for work, bus drivers are forced to meet schedules or lose their jobs, and air traffic controllers keep a sharp eye on the timing of flight landings and departures to prevent collisions. All this makes for stress.

What has this to do with ECK? This spiritual path is a true one. Proof of this is in the great

The password in ECK is change, for all living things are in flux, moving toward growth or decline.

amount of change that an ECKist experiences. The Mahanta reminds him to keep the delicate balance within himself, for unless he does, he is like a planet out of control that will collide with another and destroy both of them.

In "Perspectives on Superhealth" by Sandra McLanahan, M.D., *Complementary Medicine* (Sept.–Oct. 1986), she says, "What is the definition of stress? Originally, the word was invoked by Hans Selye to mean 'change.' He found that any change in a system, whether good or bad, creates stress."

Dr. McLanahan told the story of Paul "Bear" Bryant, who was the winningest football coach in college history. She said that "retirement is one of the most major life changes, and may put some persons at increased risk for illness." Coach Bryant, whose whole life had been football, said this to friends a day before his translation (death), just thirty-six days after retirement: "No more Saturdays." Suddenly, he had nothing more to look forward to.

Some people do not suffer from stress the way others do and therefore may enjoy better health, according to Dr. McLanahan. Travel is a bad time for stress, probably the reason for increased heart attacks from the frustrations of lost baggage, missed flights, or surly hotel staff. Higher illness rates follow a death in the family, divorce, or retirement. Dr. McLanahan draws an interesting conclusion from her research and gives a suggestion on how one may enjoy health even in times of severe stress.

She underlines the fact that the traditional view of family in Western culture has broken down. The unconditional love ("I know my spouse, sister, or brother will love me, no matter how I err") is "rare

The Mahanta reminds the ECKist to keep the delicate balance within himself, for unless he does, he is like a planet out of control that will collide with another and destroy both of them.

and seldom lasting." For one to compensate for the loss of his traditional family, she recommends that he look at the universe as a web, in which everyone is linked together. This allows for an expanded meaning of family. She proposes a way to meet the ever-faster rate of change (stress) in our family and world: Learn to experience " 'family' with every person we meet, at any moment."

How much is this like the ECK initiate who sees the Mahanta in everyone he meets. If we are such a person, then we are able to "create family—unconditional love—with the grocer, store bagger, the person we meet walking down the street, with every person we meet, with the kind of openness, connection, universal and unconditional love usually reserved for 'family.' "

Not surprisingly, she found health benefits accrue for those who practiced visualization for fifteen minutes a day. For ECK initiates, visualization is via the Spiritual Exercises of ECK, which are more restful than sleep and can possibly help control stress in one's immune and cardiovascular systems.

The rate of karma has been hurried along in the twentieth century. The faster pace has left many with a sense of loss. Familiar things are swept aside. This makes for stress and illness, and it is harder than ever for an individual to stay in balance. Signs that we are out of balance include surprising things like: there's no parking space and our temper shows, we have an argument at home, the car breaks down, we are upset by thoughtless shoppers in the food store who block the aisles with their carts, or a bird spots our freshly washed car.

But this is life. It is a spiritual opportunity for Soul to learn to serve first mankind, then Sugmad.

Look at the universe as a web, in which everyone is linked together. This allows for an expanded meaning of family.

Each individual repeatedly meets three stages in every struggle in life: (1) the need to change whatever bothers him, (2) a dark night of Soul while he flounders for direction, and (3) his eventual entrance into new and better conditions. Each creative struggle to overcome his woes moves one from a position of self-service to one of greater service to God and mankind.

How does this apply to us in ECK? A change that is made too abruptly from Christianity to ECK can throw us off center. Two years of discourse study are generally required before one can take the Second Initiation. This is to allow for a gradual change from the old values to the new ones of ECK.

But even a two-year interval of study before the Second may be too soon for some chelas. What if the pink slip for initiation comes, but he is not ready to commit his spiritual life to ECK? He may then continue his discourse study into the third year, even though he does not take the Second Initiation.

The Second Initiation is a spiritual commitment made with the Holy Spirit. It should not be taken unless one is really ready for it.

The ECK program heals an individual, allowing ample time for the new spiritual values of ECK to replace those of his former religion. It takes time. If change is brought about too fast, one loses his sense of purpose. We want to see the individual develop flexibility to meet rapidly changing conditions, and better use his imaginative resources.

All in the lower worlds is uncertainty and change. Only in the Mahanta's love is there balance. Only in him is there stability.

All in the lower worlds is uncertainty and change. Only in the Mahanta's love is there balance. Only in him is there stability.

If troubles do not bring one the capacity for love, then his whole life will have been in vain.

CHAPTER SIX

Death as a Doorway

22
LOSSES OF THE HEART

An article in *Psychology Today* reported a study that said the death of a loved one is among the things most feared by Americans. But whether it is the loss of a loved one, a serious illness, or financial worries, the lesson is that love binds all wounds. If troubles do not bring one the capacity for love, then his whole life will have been in vain.

A woman, who is not an initiate, wrote of the loss of her husband, who died at the relatively young age of sixty-one. Their marriage had been one of warmth and tenderness, rare and exquisite beyond description. He had been an exceptional man who showed love and kindness to all he met. But his translation had left her to deal with a tremendous void and a despondency that would be natural under the circumstances. She had reached a low point in her life, lost all interest in it, and now asked the Mahanta for help in overcoming the despair.

For a week, I carried her letter with me on a business trip, wondering how to respond with a letter of consolation. But when we act as clear

Whether it is the loss of a loved one, a serious illness, or financial worries, the lesson is that love binds all wounds. If troubles do not bring one the capacity for love, then his whole life will have been in vain.

channels for the ECK, It may arrange a parallel condition for us, such as a loss. Not until I had dealt with my own inner state and had gotten a perspective of the traumatic events that hit me, was I able to respond to her letter in the proper fashion.

I recommended that she visit a rest home and look for a resident whose face reflected kindliness, goodness, and humor. She was to be a pupil at the feet of a wise teacher, who might give her an understanding of how to cope with sorrow. Older people have often faced the death of loved ones. Most have somehow picked themselves up and gone on living. Perhaps the widow could too. She might find a balm for her own sorrow, as well as give it to another who needed it as much as she did.

Death for an ECK initiate is not the dark mystery that haunts the Christian. It is known that Soul exists forever and retains Its individuality when the earthly shell is dropped at death.

The activity of Soul often increases as the day of translation draws near. The night before she left the body, an ECK chela made an overseas visit to a friend, by Soul Travel, to inform her that she was about to leave the physical plane, and the next morning she did. An overseas call confirmed her passing. She had wanted to prepare the friend for this change and bid her farewell. There was no sadness for either of them.

Love is the only thing that can replace a loss of the heart, and Soul Travel is the gateway to love. Soul, as long as It is under the temporal conditions of the lower planes, will have losses of many kinds. But Soul, knowing of Its divine nature, sees beyond the ends of eternity and knows It can never be extinguished like a candle's flame.

Love is the only thing that can replace a loss of the heart, and Soul Travel is the gateway to love.

When Saint Paul said, "I die daily," he was talking of a common, everyday occurrence in his life. He meant the experience of Soul Travel, which gave him the confidence to face the threat of death on his many missionary journeys.

This initiate in Africa reported a Soul Travel experience, which is the dying daily of Saint Paul. He was taken out of the body while lying on his bed. In his inner vision, he saw the image of an irregularly shaped hexagon, inside of which was an oval. The colors of the shape kept changing from red to orange to green to deep blue—spanning the full spectrum of colors in the rainbow. All the colors were bright and vivid, but he was at a loss to explain the meaning of this experience.

Anyone who makes contact with the Sound or Light of God is really outside the body, whether he knows it or not. The rapidly changing colors seen by the chela indicated that Soul was moving up and down through the various spirito-material bodies and recording Its impressions of them. Each inner body has a distinctive color, which registered in the Spiritual Eye of the beholder. The geometric shape of the image meant that Soul was observing the bodies in a geometrical dimension from the Mental Plane.

A balance must be struck between the objective and subjective states of an individual. The widow who cries for relief from the emptiness of losing her companion will find love by giving it to someone in a rest home. But outer service is only a portion of the comprehensive healing that is available from Spirit. The other part comes through the Spiritual Exercises of ECK, which let the Essence of God come into the heart to heal the wounds of doubt, loss, and worry.

Anyone who makes contact with the Sound or Light of God is really outside the body, whether he knows it or not.

Soul Travel is of no use to anyone unless he learns to love, for love is the catalyst in the concerns of Soul. Love the Sugmad and your fellowman, if you would be the heir of heaven.

23
UNDERSTANDING DEATH

he great fear behind all fears is the fear of death. So in this Year of Spiritual Healing, we must look at the spiritual matter of translation, the death of the physical body. It has been stated that everything about death had already been said, which is partially so, but the poetic Preacher of Ecclesiastes had a most eloquent way of putting death into perspective with life when he said: "To everything there is a season, and a time to every purpose under the heaven: A time to be born, and a time to die. . . . A time to weep, and a time to laugh; a time to mourn, and a time to dance."

We think we know what detachment is until someone we dearly love translates. Then we're not so sure and wonder if the Mahanta is really with us in our sorrow.

The ancient philosophers struggled with the fact of death. Epicurus, the Greek philosopher, taught that the physical senses are infallible in determining truth. Despite that grave misunderstanding, he did make the interesting observation that "there is nothing terrible in living to a man who rightly comprehends that there is nothing terrible in

The great fear behind all fears is the fear of death.

111

ceasing to live." Lucretius, the Roman philosopher and poet, said that death should not concern us at all. He felt that when Soul left the body, It ceased to exist: life swallowed up in death. A hopeless and gloomy philosophy if ever there was one.

But for us in ECK, the bleak night of materialistic philosophy is shattered by the lightning of ECK. Soul is free; a marvelous particle of God. The Sound and Light of the Sugmad shine within It, without beginning or end, beyond eternity.

Here we enter the picture and look through the eyes of Soul. The golden curtain of God is drawn back, and we are suspended for a moment above time and space. Below us swirl magnificent universes, pinpoints of light in a sea of darkness. But none of the constellations in any of the galaxies can compare with the Sound and Light that dress Soul in the golden land of Sat Nam.

Soul enters into the material universe, which in the end conditions It to serve the Sugmad with boundless love.

Then Soul has the sensation of falling a great distance, the golden light dims, and the individual awakens as a baby crying in the arms of its mother on one of the distant specks of light. Thus Soul enters into the material universe, which in the end conditions It to serve the Sugmad with boundless love.

The individual matures and dies; his atoms return to dust. Before long, the Lords of Karma stir the dust to create a new body for him, and the wheel of life begins another turn.

How does the ECK initiate's translation differ from that of a noninitiate? First, the Angel of Death no longer has power over him; second, the Mahanta guides him past the Lords of Karma; third, translation is an initiation into the Sound and Light of ECK.

The Mahanta is Lord of all worlds and escorts his disciple on the journey through the frontiers of death. The journey is a joyful one, for the Mahanta comes to the initiate in the last moments and says, "Are you ready, my beloved?" There is no hesitation, for the individual is delighted to see his old friend and is helped out of the rumpled clothing of his physical body. The Sound and Light of the Mahanta surround him, and they begin a leisurely passage through pastures of flowers and along serene riverbanks.

Therefore, the chela is never alone for a moment but is greeted immediately by the Mahanta at the time of translation. There is no waiting in the courtyard of the King of the Dead, for the all-powerful Master is by his side. Do not grieve for those who die in ECK, for they are the most fortunate of all.

An ECK initiate tells of her encounter with death. She got the flu, and her fever climbed to a serious level. Suddenly, the Angel of Death appeared at her bedside, but, just as quickly, the Mahanta was there and said, "She is my chela; you have no power over her." Then to her, he said, "Come, it's time to go," and they stepped into the white Light.

This experience was to answer two questions for her: (1) Does Soul retain any connection with the body after death, and (2) is there any pain during cremation?

As she stood beside Wah Z, the Mahanta, he showed her how Soul left the body as white light. Indeed, a complete separation of Soul from the physical body took place. How could there be pain in cremation without a connection between body and Soul? She realized that only through Soul can the physical and all other bodies experience life

As she stood beside Wah Z, the Mahanta, he showed her how Soul left the body as white light.

here in the lower worlds. She was not separated
from herself but was fully conscious as she stood
beside the Master. The plight of the physical body
did not concern her in the least.

Then she saw her husband's vigil by her sick-
bed. She felt such great love for him and could sense
his loneliness and despair. Her light wrapped around
him to ease his pain. The Mahanta saw this great
love she had for her husband and said to her, "You
can stay because you already have a heart of gold."
But she hesitated and said, "Beloved Mahanta, while
I love my husband beyond anything that I know,
you come always first. And if you say I must go with
you, I will."

The Master then said to her: "Love is the greatest power there is. Because you love so much, I will
let you return to the physical body. You will, of
course, have great pain with this sickness, a pain
that need not be but is your choice." The Mahanta
gives choices which the Angel of Death cannot give.

Before returning her to the physical body, the
Mahanta took her into the inner planes and showed
her such secrets as the source of all creations in the
lower planes. They stood in the Blue Light, and he
said, "This is where all creations start. We are at
the beginning of life." Before she reentered her
fevered body, he said, "You are being returned and,
in exchange, must give total service to the ECK."
When she got into the body, she was very sick but
soon recovered.

A humorous sidelight is that the next night the
Angel of Death came again and stood by her bed.
He said, "I'd love to take you, but I have no power
over you." The dark angel had just come to have a
last look.

The Mahanta saw this great love she had for her husband and said to her, "You can stay because you already have a heart of gold." The Mahanta gives choices which the Angel of Death cannot give.

Grief is for those who stay behind. The Soul that is freed of the body delights in the Sound and Light, and in the fullness of being. Now It wants nothing more than to serve the Infinite, the Sugmad.

24
ENDINGS ARE BEGINNINGS

*J*f Eckankar can offer people anything, it's how to get over the fear of death. A woman, who found ECK during Paul Twitchell's time, disagreed with her former church's teaching that the dead remained unconscious in a black grave until Judgment Day. In her heart, she simply knew that was untrue. She began a search for books on reincarnation in bookstores and libraries. "Do you know how few books there were on reincarnation twenty years ago?" she asked. But Paul's message of ECK gave her a hope such as she had never thought to find. He said that Soul is eternal, and that whoever is on "the high path of ECK always dwells in the spiritual planes."

The consciousness of the public has indeed become broader since then, but death still alarms people. A common belief is that both the good and the evil are in their graves until the Last Day. This means that any of our loved ones who have passed on—father, mother, brother, or sister—are not in heaven at all, but in the ground. Job, the Old Testament figure, must still be there, waiting patiently, thirty-five centuries later.

Soul is eternal and whoever is on the high path of ECK always dwells in the spiritual planes.

117

When I was in college, a pop-psychology quiz made the rounds among the students. The idea was to unlock an individual's unconscious feelings about life and death. One question was, "You come to a wall in the woods. What kind of a wall do you see, and can you get over it?" Unknown to those who took the test, the wall was to signify death. Responses were on this order: (1) "I see a castle wall— and you must be kidding, nobody gets over that!" (2) "It is an earthen wall that reaches to my chest. I could get over it if I tried." or (3) "There is a low rock wall covered with ivy; it's easy to get over, but the dirt on it makes it messy."

Death is but one line in the Book of Life. Life expands forever into greater circles; death is just a springboard.

Any who are like those in the first group see death as an insurmountable obstacle. Fear, no doubt, rules them, and they miss much of the enjoyment that life offers. For those in the second group, death is a minor challenge, but they are sure to go through the experience fairly well when it comes. The people in the last group are not at all frightened. Death is an event of slight inconvenience in the continuity of life. Death is but one line in the Book of Life. Life expands forever into greater circles; death is just a springboard.

Many years ago, a woman suffered a serious accident and was pronounced clinically dead. During her absence from the body, she went to a place where nine men around a table (ECK Masters) made a decision to heal her crushed lungs so she could return to earth and accomplish what she had come here to do. They did not heal all her injuries but enough of them so she could go on with her spiritual unfoldment. She was given a new lease on life because this was the lifetime she was to make great spiritual gains that would not be possible under easier conditions.

Then, five years ago, the Mahanta again took her out of the body, this time to the Causal Plane, where a guardian let her read her past-life records. This spiritual being was so gentle and loving that she begged to remain, but he said it was necessary for her to return to her body. Her learning would be speeded up so that she would never have to return to another earthly life after this one.

Death is simply the end of something in a known form that reappears as a new beginning. There are more aspects to death than the demise of the physical body. Another variation of death is the end of a relationship. This is usually a painful time for one or the other of the two parties, but the spiritual help of the Mahanta is there, if one should ask for it and can accept it.

A man wrote that he loved a woman who did not return his love. Until then, he had been certain that he could calmly accept any test from the Master, but this situation left him helpless, on the verge of an emotional breakdown. When he was about to break, he finally thought to ask the Mahanta for help while in contemplation. On the inner planes, he was put on a beautiful old sailing ship without sails that was moored near a sandy beach. This was his dream boat, but the mast empty of sails meant that all he wanted or desired in this relationship was going nowhere. On the mast was a button, which if he pushed it, would blow up and destroy all his lovely dreams. But he had to do it if he wanted any peace, even though it would be painful to shatter his dreams.

So he pushed the button, destroyed the old ship, and watched it sink to the bottom of the sea, never to rise again. When he realized the finality of his

Death is simply the end of something in a known form that reappears as a new beginning.

deed, he became quite emotional, and for a moment he experienced intense sorrow and loss. But then, unexpectedly, came the feeling of freedom and relaxation; his burden lifted. The Mahanta, who was his companion in this drama, then lifted him to a higher level of consciousness and led him into "a rich, green, warm, bright land" that the ECK initiate was ready to explore now.

This was a profound spiritual experience that left him detached about that relationship, because he knew it was up to him to do something about it, one way or the other—if he wished. The end of a relationship, like all endings, is really the beginning of a new spiritual chapter for us.

The key to survival here and in the afterlife is the ability to yield. *The Shariyat* says that "he who can yield, can survive both here in life and in the invisible worlds." This means letting go of old ideas such as what supposedly happens to Soul after the death of the body. It's also learning how to regain serenity when our routines are shaken up and we are bruised.

The key to survival here and in the afterlife is the ability to yield. This means letting go of old ideas such as what supposedly happens to Soul after the death of the body.

What is the golden thread between our daily life and the spiritual worlds? *The Shariyat-Ki-Sugmad* tells us the right kind of worship is simply an expression of our love and adoration.

CHAPTER SEVEN

Sharing the ECK Teachings

25

A TRUE UNDERSTANDING OF WORSHIP

*A*chela wrote a letter to me about worship, which is becoming a more prominent feature of Eckankar. Before ECK, she had been a Roman Catholic, and that prompted her reaction to this development. In the meantime, however, she has made peace with herself. Yet she wonders, *Perhaps people should know the Mahanta, the Living ECK Master is making these changes to uplift the terms* worship *and* religion *for everyone. Maybe people would find it easier to accept them.* She understands that we are here to be a Co-worker with God, not for self-glorification.

Mankind has trampled worship into dust, making of it a tired and worn celebration of God's human messengers. The Sugmad has thus sent the Mahanta, the Living ECK Master to restore a true understanding of worship to all religions. Worship, when rightly done, is a love song to God.

The Shariyat-Ki-Sugmad clears up mistaken ideas about worship. People often misuse worship, thinking it an easy route to material gifts. "In many of the metaphysical and psychic teachings," says *The Shariyat*, "the religious aspect or the worship

Worship, when rightly done, is a love song to God.

*To worship
God in hopes
of a return is
a negative act.*

of the Supreme Deity is lost and they become merely
a method of mental manipulation for purely personal gains, though not necessarily and deliber-
ately evil."

To worship God in hopes of a return is a negative act. Who do such people actually worship? "Many
religions worship this force [the Universal Mind, or
Kal power] as the true spirit," continues *The
Shariyat*, "and their followers are always in trouble
whether they pray for material things or to God for
the many things which are needed to make up
living on earth. It gives only temporary relief and
must be avoided at all cost by the ECKist who
wants the true reality of the Sugmad."

Another misguided worship is that of God's messengers. People in the human state of awareness
often cannot tell whether someone has a high or low
state of consciousness. Therefore, they fall into a
trap that keeps their minds from truth. Book One
of *The Shariyat* reads: "The trouble with religion is
that one individual appears in what might be a
perfect manifestation of God, and so begins a worship of that manifestation. Most of these manifes-
tations are only social, Astral, or Mental phenomena
and they deceive the worshiper."

Well, then, who or what do we worship?

Certainly not the physical form of the Living
ECK Master. Listen to Book One: "The Mahanta is
a law unto himself. So oft does he speak of life itself
as being his servant, but he commands heaven and
earth, yet never does he allow himself to be wor-
shiped perfectly as man. Only as the Mahanta, the
perfect consciousness."

Our spiritual goal must be to enter the "eternal
becoming" of ECK. This quest begins within us. Of

this, Book Two of *The Shariyat* says: "Starting from the same point of departure in the unknowable, this journey is the worship of and the search for the ECK within man himself, and the return of man to the Sugmad, the Godhead."

What is the golden thread between our daily life and the spiritual worlds?

"The very form of the chela's life is a fore-shadowing of the life of heaven and those high worlds," states *The Shariyat*, Book Two. "It is primarily a life of worship and adoration, for all ECKists must live a life in the Spiritual Exercises of ECK, which brings about the simplicity of living in joy and happiness. At the heart of the ECK life lies the conviction that the ECK is the way as well as the goal."

And it continues: "There will be many within the body, who, if they are doing the tasks to which they are spiritually called, will have little time for the conscious offering of the spiritual contemplation and worship of Sugmad. Because this is so, such active lives are not second best but just as valid as any other vocation within the whole body of the Mahanta."

Other passages from *The Shariyat-Ki-Sugmad* tell us more about the right kind of worship: It is simply an expression of our love and adoration. The Sugmad, the ECK, or the Mahanta do not ask anyone to worship them. True love gives freely. Our love for them returns many times over.

True love gives freely.

In *The Spiritual Notebook*, Paul Twitchell makes the observation, "Contemplation is getting very close to the highest form of worship, for it carries the practitioner beyond the Mental planes and into the Fifth, or Soul, Plane."

That hints at the ECK definition of worship.

Although outer forms will pass away, rightly used they can express our love for God.

What, then, are some common forms of worship? *World Religions*, edited by Geoffrey Parrinder, outlines these:

1. Prayer

2. Sacrifice
   a. gift or offering
   b. harvest festival

3. Rituals
   a. through sacred dramas
   b. in sacred places

However, true prayer or worship is content with the workings of God. It does not seek to change conditions or events. The ECK blessing, "Baraka Bashad," and the HU Song are examples of the highest spiritual forms of prayer or worship.

True prayer or worship is content with the workings of God. It does not seek to change conditions or events.

26

Loopholes for Locked Consciousness

A recent trip to South Africa and Europe brought to bear certain circumstances that bind Souls in different countries. You, the initiates, must find the resources to decipher the particular lock that is placed upon the people in your home communities. What is standing between them and the message of ECK, which many of them want but are afraid to seek?

Greece provides an interesting study of a place that is made so comfortable with the support of family ties that few yearn to find what lies beyond this life. The Souls that have incarnated there have created a haven so agreeable to their need for physical contentment, that they have eliminated any desire for the worlds of God beyond.

The golden age of Greece occurred roughly from 630–330 BC. This period of unparalleled cultural activity saw the building of the Parthenon under the guidance of the Living ECK Master of the times, Phidias, who was more directly in charge of the sculptures.

During the time of ancient Greece, there came

129

into being the famed Oracle of Delphi, located on the lower slopes of Mt. Parnassus. At that time this was considered the center of the world. It is even as Paul Twitchell said, "The Oracle still speaks for those who have the ears to hear." I also found this to be true, as the Oracle laid out matters of deep concern to me, but also gave the means to handle them.

In its earliest history, the master spoke to the disciple, the initiate. Conversation was via the inner channels, including the dream state. Time marched on, and the site at Delphi gained in popularity with people other than initiates.

Now the Oracle degenerated to a form of mediumship marshaled by the priests as a control device over ignorant devotees. A woman, under the influence of an entity, sat in an underground room purporting to be the instrument through which spoke the great voice of Apollo.

Time passed and popular demand grew so great that the priests added two more oracles to the original one to handle the crowds. Supplicants camped outside the Oracle for days and weeks, waiting for word that the great Oracle would see them.

Unknown to them, while they contemplated upon the sacred grounds, the supplicants were being interviewed for their suitability as conversants with the voice of Apollo. In the meantime, they innocently divulged bits and pieces of their problems to informants of the priests, and the most appropriate cases were selected for an audience with the esteemed Oracle.

Strangely enough, as the crowds descended upon the site, the din of the carnival atmosphere began to drown out the true voice of the Deity. But the

In its earliest history, the master spoke to the disciple, the initiate. Conversation was via the inner channels, including the dream state.

lower psychic forces were ready to step into place immediately and fulfill the needs of the ignorant. Thus the true voice of the Oracle stopped its prophecies long before the crowds finally shrank away decades later.

Another kind of control by the churchly hierarchy is in motion today. This is the spiritual atmosphere that binds the community where each of you lives. The form taken is different in each locality, but the end result is the same: to blind and bind Soul to the comforts and delusions of mortality.

A correspondent in Germany says that the state collects a church tax there for the churches. One becomes a registered member of either the Catholic or Protestant church at birth. He stays that unless he resigns officially at a government office. A decision to leave the mother church is a mark upon the forehead, a sign of shame in the smaller communities. Whoever secedes officially from the church is barred from church weddings and funerals, a frightening prospect to the people.

Although the churches are empty on Sundays, millions of paying "tax Christians" secure their place in heaven by staying registered members and filling the cash box of the churches. The church knows that every lost member means lost revenue. Since cash is the fuel of power, the church officials don't care whether their temples are empty or not. They care only about the bank account.

In Italy the situation is somewhat different. An ECK member who travels there frequently observes that the country is remarkably conservative. It is a closed society where only the closest family and friends are invited into a home.

Another kind of control by the churchly hierarchy is in motion today to blind and bind Soul to the comforts and delusions of mortality.

The appeal of the ECK works is the *personalness* of the chela's relationship with the Mahanta, the Living ECK Master. They have a great fear that their neighbors will find out their involvement with Eckankar. The most attractive part of the ECK teachings is the one-on-one relationship between them and the Master. Also, they can realize God now without a priest or church atmosphere, in the words of the ECK correspondent.

Each one of you is looking for a loophole through which the frightened and locked-in consciousness of people can escape to find the Light and Sound of God.

This means that each one of you is looking for a loophole through which the frightened and locked-in consciousness of people can escape to find the Light and Sound of God.

The value of the spiritual exercises is that each one of you can independently find the proper way to give service to the Mahanta because of your immediate communication with him every day. This inner connection is totally unknown to the religionists who follow the major orthodox teachings. This *modus operandi*, however, is the strength of the transmission of the gospel of ECK throughout the current times.

I am always with you through your own efforts to reach God Consciousness in this lifetime.

27
WHERE YOU FIT IN, IN ECK

he RESA program is birthed. Like any child, it must trip and fall in the beginning, because that is how one learns to walk. Each step is a wobbly gamble, a decided risk. But walking gives strength; and strength, assurance.

With the emergence of the RESA program, time will see Eckankar become more of an outer and an inner path. On the surface, it may appear much like other religions. To survive on the battlefield of the material world, however, it must adopt the attire, the armor, that is the current fashion. But the inner teaching will always remain the Path of Sound and Light. Sooner or later—hopefully much later—people in Eckankar may separate like cream from milk into the true followers and the institutionalists. The true followers will be guided by love; the latter, by the blinding narcotic of power.

The RESA field structure is only meant to be an instrument of the ECK to present Its message to humanity. Yet already there are initiates who regard the program as their ladder to personal recognition. The RESAs have a hard enough time trying to balance the conflicting forces within their areas

Sooner or later— hopefully much later— people in Eckankar may separate like cream from milk into the true followers and the institutionalists. The true followers will be guided by love; the latter, by the blinding narcotic of power.

without having to contend with this. When Jesus said to his disciples, "One of you shall betray me," all in turn asked, "Lord, is it I?" Eleven were faithful; only one was not.

This is not to discourage anyone. The birthing of a baby, a nation, a spiritual path, or a structure within it—all have unimaginable difficulties. But hardships do not mean we would desert a baby, abandon a nation, forget the spiritual path, or not support its structure. Uncertainty is a part of growing up. A child, even a nation, makes errors. What counts are the lessons learned from them. If love is allowed to infuse the RESA program, it will be an entirely different structure than if power is its driving force. Love overlooks, forgives. Power is self-righteous and vengeful.

Love overlooks, forgives. Power is self-righteous and vengeful.

There must be capable administrators in the RESA program if Eckankar is to be an effective instrument for presenting the message of ECK. Not everyone has the skills. There must also be good Arahatas. It requires a special talent to teach others: not all have it. And there must also be those who walk among the public without ever speaking directly about ECK, because not all people are ready to hear of the ECK teachings directly. But whatever you do well, do it. Let others serve with their special gifts. If the RESA program lives up to its intended purpose, it will give every chela an opportunity to unfold along the lines of his spiritual interests. Then Eckankar will really have something to offer people.

To reach high positions of service, all ECK leaders must show integrity, be expansive in their vision, and above all, they must have humility. A tall order.

A correspondent expressed the desire to teach others about the true God, Sugmad, but he could not do it in the guise of a preacher, even if it was for ECK. The way he felt most comfortable in being an ECK channel was to visit with people in towns and in the country. He would enjoy their company and likely never speak the word *ECK*. He wondered if that could be enough to qualify him as a carrier of ECK. Certainly.

Other kinds of service involve the Arahata. In the early days of Eckankar, Second Initiates who showed a desire and gift for teaching were given the opportunity to teach. What was missing in polish they made up for in love. This suggests that Higher Initiates be willing to allow new Second Initiates to take Arahata training, and do all they can to support the new ECK teachers. If complaints do arise about a certain teacher, and retraining proves unsuccessful, the individual can be given other duties that better fit his abilities. Generally there is a way to do this kindly.

An aside in regard to Satsang classes: a picture of the Mahanta, the Living ECK Master in the Satsang room is of spiritual benefit to the class and visitors.

Another way to be a channel for ECK is as an unsung hospice worker. The blessings in this line of service are almost beyond words. An ECKist, a hospice worker, was assigned to a woman in her fifties who was dying of cancer. Doctors had given her less than six months to live. When her weight dropped below a hundred pounds, everyone thought the end was near. The ECK initiate visited her with the attitude of being a channel in whatever way the ECK wanted. When she was with the patient, she

Second Initiates who showed a desire and gift for teaching were given the opportunity to teach. What was missing in polish they made up for in love.

The outer and inner teachings of ECK come from the same source, and it is necessary for all in ECK to find this center point of balance within their own hearts and minds.

was just a friend. They never spoke about spiritual matters and seldom of her impending death. When the ECKist reached the woman's house early in the morning, she always took the opportunity to do a spiritual exercise, leaving the patient's situation and her job there in the hands of the ECK.

Then an unusual thing happened. The patient's condition began to improve, and she gained weight. This baffled the doctors, who chalked up her improvement to an unexplained miracle of modern medicine. But the ECKist knew better. The ECK had intervened, perhaps because the patient lived each day with gratitude and love.

There is a place for everyone in Eckankar. What is necessary now is for all to practice charity toward others, and especially themselves. The outer and inner teachings of ECK come from the same source, and it is necessary for all in ECK to find this center point of balance within their own hearts and minds. That remains the simplest and most enriching road to Mastership.

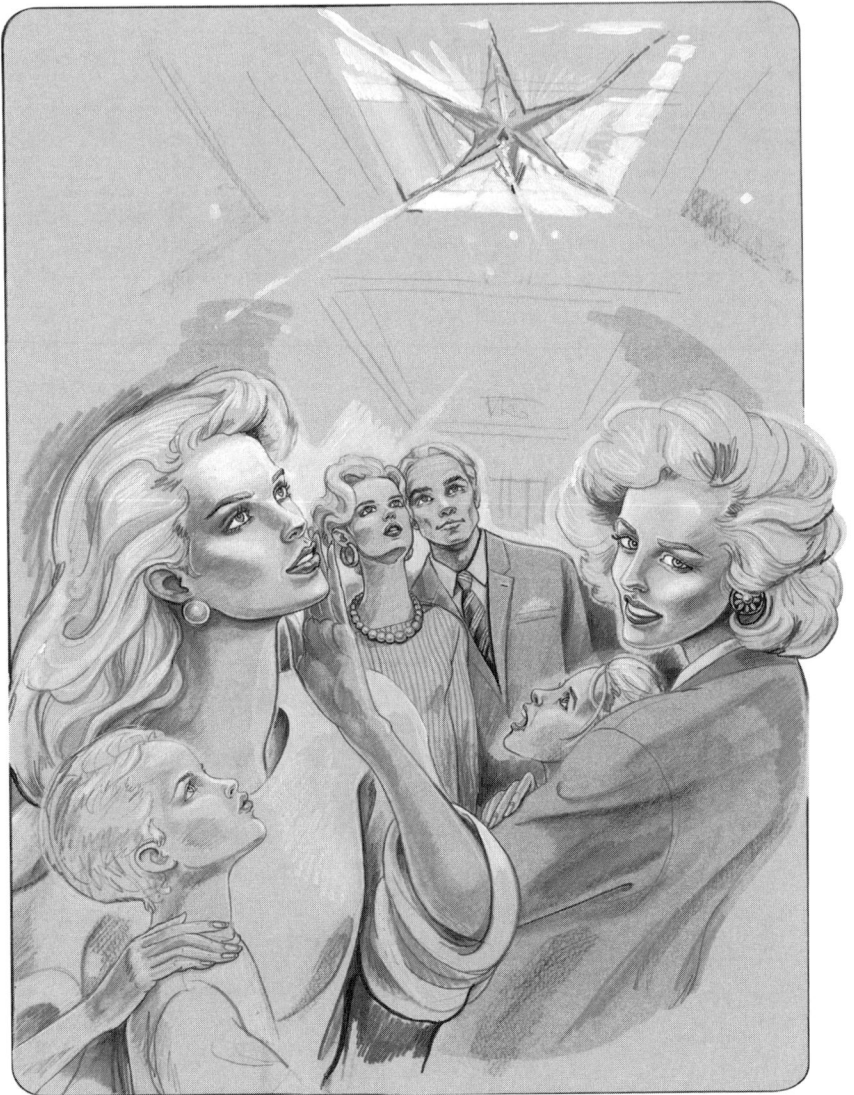

Dedicate yourself to the Sugmad when you come to the Temple of ECK. That is and will always be the most important dedication of all.

CHAPTER EIGHT

The Temple of ECK

28

APPROACHING THE TEMPLE

The dedication of the Temple of ECK is a historic moment in the spiritual history of mankind. I would have liked to have had everyone at the dedication who wanted to come. Of course, this idea was out of the question because of limited space.

So it became necessary to look at the dedication of the Temple in a new light. While that event was momentous, another will be far greater: the inner dedication of each of you who comes to the Temple of ECK. All who approach the ECK Temple in purity and in light will find the blessings of God enter their lives. The dedication thus becomes a personal consecration. Every time you enter the Temple of ECK, make and renew your commitment to the ways of ECK. Dedicate yourself as a Co-worker with the Mahanta. In doing so, you will bring others to the Light and Sound of God through your words and deeds. This personal commitment is the most meaningful dedication of all.

While in Europe this summer, I took the opportunity to visit the medieval cathedral at Chartres, France. It is a beautiful structure, known for its

All who approach the ECK Temple in purity and in light will find the blessings of God enter their lives.

stained-glass windows. The cathedral, set in a small city, is mainly a tourist attraction; otherwise, it would have little use at all. It and the churches in Europe are mostly empty on Sunday. This fact disturbs the clergy there, because Europe is the cradle of the Reformation. What has gone awry with the Reformation in Europe? What has gone wrong with Christianity? And what is the matter with many of the religions in the world that members gain so little peace and love?

Mostly, the ancient, necessary doctrines of God's Light and Sound have slowly fallen into disuse and into a dark age of spiritual ignorance. It is ironic, but such is the case. People too much caught up in the spell of modern living don't notice a vacuum in their lives. That missing something is the Spirit of God.

We know this Spirit of God as the ECK. Other names for It include the Sound Current, the Audible Life Stream, the Music of God, and many other expressions. The worshipers in orthodox religions have heard of It as the Holy Spirit. Yet, their own religions give so little spiritual direction that few have ever tasted this divine nectar.

The Light and Sound are the most sure way to the love of God.

The Light and Sound are the most sure way to the love of God. So many speak about God's love today, but few, if any, really know its meaning. God is love, and the way to it is through the Sound and Light. What could be simpler?

And yet, the direct path to God's love remains a riddle for most. It is not simply giving charity to the weak and sick, because those acts are but a small part of divine love expressing itself. The love of God is something else entirely. It is a willingness to put all life and its creatures on an equal footing with us. And such a willingness is not from some human act of charity, but from a love of the divine essence within all beings.

So in the cathedral at Chartres, I saw a mighty building that had once tried to serve the spiritual needs of the community. Now, however, it is mostly for tourists. Most visitors come mainly to admire the design and construction, artifacts, and stained glass. At that level, there is some beauty, of course. Yet, some pilgrims at Chartres must hope for something more: a spiritual connection. I doubt that many find it.

The Temple of ECK is not nearly so large as the building at Chartres, but it will serve the spiritual needs of people better. Those who come to the ECK Temple with pure hearts will find truth in dreams. Others will come to know the spiritual reasons for everyday events. Still others will find what they could find nowhere else: the beginnings of truth and wisdom while still on earth. The Temple of ECK has a destiny to fulfill, and you can help.

Let people know about the Light and Sound of God. Also tell them about HU, the ancient name for God that has the power to heal. Many will turn away, but those who have already met the Mahanta inwardly will want to know more. Make yourself a clear channel for God. Be a channel in your own way.

Let people know about the Light and Sound of God. Also tell them about HU, the ancient name for God that has the power to heal.

So come to the Temple of ECK. But first purify yourself in a waterfall of Light and Sound. Then watch your heart while in the Temple to see the effect of divine love upon you. Continue to watch when you are home again, to see how the ECK works Its wonders in and through you.

Dedicate yourself to the Sugmad when you come to the Temple of ECK. That is and will always be the most important dedication of all.

29
ARE YOU WILLING TO SERVE ALL LIFE?

*N*ow is a fitting time to reflect upon what the Temple of ECK means for each initiate.

The ECK Temple represents the union between one's goal of spiritual freedom and the need to then become a Co-worker with God. This twofold approach to the spiritual life hinges upon the enlightened one's willingness to serve all living creatures. In practice, such service works out to leadership in ECK.

You are a leader in ECK. Although many levels and positions of leadership exist, every leader must deal with responsibility and accountability. These two terms naturally involve a third: delegation. Let's see how they relate to the Temple of ECK, your mission as a Co-worker with God, and harmony in your personal life.

To begin, the new Temple of ECK is simply a building. As with every physical element, it will someday turn to dust. As long as it stands, however, it must be a distribution point for the spiritual energies of ECK to flood the world.

The ECK Temple represents the union between one's goal of spiritual freedom and the need to then become a Co-worker with God.

Our physical bodies are likewise temples. Both they and the Temple of ECK are centers through which the ECK passes to reach people in search of truth.

We, in our human bodies, are little temples. Looking at it from another view, we are like satellites in orbit around the celestial body of the ECK teachings. Leaders in ECK must learn to use their talents wisely. So let me briefly pass along to you three mainstays of leadership: responsibility, accountability, and delegation.

Let me briefly pass along to you three mainstays of leadership: responsibility, accountability, and delegation.

Here are the definitions of these three words as I recently gave them to the RESAs. For example, the Sugmad has given (delegated) to me the mission (responsibility) of gathering up Souls to help them return to the Ocean of Love and Mercy. However, the job is too big for me to do alone. I now look for capable people to share the responsibility. So far we've covered two of the three mainstays of leadership: responsibility and delegation.

Not long ago Millie Moore, Eighth Initiate, came to me with an idea. "I would like to gather and distribute used ECK books to people who can't afford new ones."

"If you can do this with volunteers," I said, "go ahead. The staff at the ECK Office is too busy with other duties." Millie agreed to the conditions. Before she left, she said, "At the next seminar, I'll give you a list of books we've given away." That's accountability.

Since then, Millie has found others to help her gather and distribute used ECK books. When someone offers to send used books, but then forgets to send them as promised, Millie holds them to account. "Where are the books you promised?" she may ask. "I thought I could count on you." That's acCOUNTability. Can a leader count on someone for help with a responsibility?

Yet conditions in our lives change. Let's say you told Millie you'd collect used books. In the meantime, however, the needs of your family require you to take on a second job. You won't be able to keep your promise. Well, tell Millie! That's accountability too. Millie can then look for someone else.

Let's go back to the purpose of this Wisdom Note. First, it was to show how responsibility, accountability, and delegation are essential to leadership in ECK. Second, what is the connection between the Temple of ECK, the initiate, and harmony in his or her personal life?

Both the Temple of ECK and our bodies are sacred. They are both to be dedicated as channels for the Sound Current, to help the Mahanta with his mission. His mission is to return those Souls who are ready to the Kingdom of God.

Yet, we must recognize our limits when giving such service. If we overwork ourselves for the cause of ECK and lose the rhythm of life, we are doing a disservice to both ourselves and everyone else.

Do the Spiritual Exercises of ECK to restore the rhythm of ECK within you.

Therefore, to be a leader in ECK also means to be kind to ourselves. Don't treat your body like a mule by overloading it. Get rest. Take care of your family. Do the Spiritual Exercises of ECK to restore the rhythm of ECK within you. Once refreshed, you can again help in the ECK Satsang classes, or wherever your talents direct.

You can only serve the ECK well if you treat your human temple kindly. It is a temple of ECK too. Be in rhythm with life, for that is to be in love

Only those who love life can serve it well.

with life. Only those who love life can serve it well.

At its dedication, the Temple of ECK also becomes the Seat of Power. It will be where the spiritual energies of all initiates of ECK will come together. The Temple will be a center for spiritual freedom and love. All who approach it in the physical, dream, or Soul body must enter with the spirit of divine love.

The Temple of ECK will allow us to reach many people with the ECK teachings, in a way we haven't done before.

30
COMMUNITY IN SPIRIT

hat is war but the collision of ideas?
Eckankar plans to build a Temple of ECK
in a suburb of Minneapolis. Then it runs
head-on into religious bigotry from certain people
in that community. This resistance is from a few men
and women who really don't live up to the teachings
of Christ on love.

History shows how Christianity, at first a victim
of persecution, later abused its authority and itself
became an oppressor. Bigotry is like a thistle seed,
waiting for a chance to grow and wound whoever
treads on it. It cannot forgive. Yet someone who
loves God, whatever his religion may be, lets others
approach God in their own way. Such generosity is
a tribute to an individual's religion.

Moment by moment, we in ECK try to live the
highest principles of divine Light and Sound. The
ECK teachings, however, do not say, "Be like sheep."
We are on the cutting edge of life. If someone is
unjust toward us, we face that injustice and try to
correct the situation by peaceful means. Yet no one
tells us to be a punching bag for the spiritually
unconscious. If forced to protect our rights in court,

*Moment by
moment, we
in ECK try
to live the
highest
principles of
divine Light
and Sound.*

we do so. Whatever the outcome of our battle, we leave it in the hands of ECK, the Holy Spirit. And many people will hear of ECK through this.

People lash out at what they fear, and fear what they don't understand. Soul Travel frightens them. They fail to realize it is one of several ways for us to experience the Light and Sound of the Holy Spirit. Such unawareness is no surprise, since our society uses up so much of its time on entertainment. Little is spent on spiritual research. Few people truly pray. Prayer is often a quick fix, insurance against the Judgment should they die in their sleep. Yet they are proud of talking to God (prayer), when maybe listening (contemplation) would be more in order.

To draw a fine line, Soul Travel is different from the expansion of consciousness. Soul Travel is a part of the whole, while the expansion of consciousness is the whole. Soul Travel is one way the Mahanta, the Living ECK Master may speed up the unfoldment of an individual. Other ways include dreams, the Golden-tongued Wisdom, events in family or business life, or a spiritual realization. Yet each of these is only a part of the expansion of consciousness.

Life carries all people and beings onward to the expansion of consciousness. For those outside of ECK, life is usually a winding road lined with blind alleys. This route to God, the Wheel of the Eighty-Four, is a slow journey due to Soul's many lives in the lower universes. The Physical, Astral, Causal, and Mental Planes are the rooms where Soul toils in God's school.

Experiences in the Sound and Light of God, however, accelerate Soul's unfoldment. The HU Song,

Soul Travel is one way the Mahanta, the Living ECK Master may speed up the unfoldment of an individual.

singing a holy name for God, sets these spiritual experiences into motion. Some people then find a better recall of their dreams, while the Mahanta lifts others directly into the heavens by Soul Travel. Each experience expands their consciousness.

Why an ECK Temple? It's not just a question of establishing one ECK Temple. In the inner worlds, there are many ECK Temples of Golden Wisdom where Souls come to learn of the Light and Sound of God. Someday there will also be ECK temples in large cities and small communities, throughout the physical world. They are necessary to establish Eckankar on earth as a spiritual teaching of the highest order. These ECK temples will be a place for truth seekers to find and learn the ancient wisdom of ECK. For this reason, we are seeing the development of a spiritual practice: the expanded HU Song for the public.

The format for the expanded HU Song for the public is: read, sing, and discuss. The history of Eckankar has seen the development of three units, or cells, of spiritual practice. First is the practice of a Satsang that meets to read from *The Shariyat-Ki-Sugmad* or from a book by the Living ECK Master. The second unit, or cell, of spiritual practice is the HU Chant. The third is the discussion class. The expanded HU Song includes all three of these elements at one meeting. The public will come to know this as the ECK Worship Service. The regular HU Chant of today will be lifted to the inner circles.

What can a spiritual traveler expect to find in the other worlds? In ECK, we can travel to the inner planes while still in our physical bodies. Our experiences there help us to handle our problems through knowledge and spiritual healing.

Some people then find a better recall of their dreams, while the Mahanta lifts others directly into the heavens by Soul Travel. Each experience expands their consciousness.

Consider the findings of this ECKist from Alaska. The Mahanta took him to a clinic in the Temple of Golden Wisdom on the Mental Plane. It is a special counseling and treatment center for depressed chelas. There, the ECK Masters sit down and talk to those in need of help. When giving therapy, the Adepts bathe the chelas in light of various colors. The colors are mostly blue and purple, but occasionally bright greens, oranges, whites, and yellows. The patient sees certain of his past lives by the ECK-Vidya, to show the cause of his depression.

Lai Tsi, the Chinese ECK Master who sometimes visits this clinic, let the ECKist from Alaska see a few unflattering traits from the past. The ECKist had shown a short temper and even cruelty toward servants who were slow to satisfy his whims. Lai Tsi said, "Study the cycles in your life. The ECK will help you handle your karma in less painful ways." He also suggested the ECKist continue to visit the clinic.

The Mahanta helps people with all their needs, but he cares most about their spiritual welfare. Life begins with HU, the holy name of God. Spend time each day in contemplation, for that is the surest way to experience the Light and Sound of God. These are the mysteries of ECK.

Life begins with HU, the holy name of God. Spend time each day in contemplation, for that is the surest way to experience the Light and Sound of God.

Acceptance of the Rod of ECK Power is an initiation where instructions come directly from the Source of Life Itself.

CHAPTER NINE

When Changes
Come in ECK

31
PASSING THE ROD
OF ECK POWER

*J*n this letter I will review what happens
when the Living ECK Master passes the
Rod of Power to his successor and what this
means to you. The rite for this transfer is a spiritual
occasion that sanctions duties of ECK Adepts along
every stratum in the divine kingdom. But it all starts
at the top.

The Master's eternal message is: "I lift you up
unto myself." During his term as chief agent for the
will of Sugmad, the Living ECK Master gathers up
Souls from the hells of materialism and prepares
them for the rites of purification. All seekers get
simple instructions in how to reach the ECK force
via the inner channels.

His mission completed, the Living ECK Master
announces his successor and passes to him the Rod
of ECK Power if he is to carry more responsibility
than is required of the Maharaji, an appointed
Master. With goodwill, the eternal play is reenacted
as the outgoing Master retires to the background.
Fubbi Quantz is an outstanding example of a former
spiritual head of the ECK Adepts who now serves

*The Master's
eternal
message is:
"I lift you up
unto myself."*

quietly out of the limelight at other duties under the present Living ECK Master.

The new Living ECK Master, upon acceptance of his mission, is given recognition in the Order of Vairagi Adepts as the key vehicle for the primordial Mahanta. This part has no personality but is only the sublime ECK in expression at the highest level.

The acceptance of the Rod of ECK Power is an initiation where instructions come directly from the Source of Life Itself. Henceforth the will of the Sugmad determines the new Living ECK Master's actions on a grand scale. This rite is the marriage of the macrocosm and the microcosm in him.

He comes to give solace and love to the tired and poor, but never in any instance will an evolved spiritual Master ever descend in a state of consciousness to reach anyone—he always *lifts* Soul into the greater stream of activity.

Never in any instance will an evolved spiritual Master ever descend in a state of consciousness to reach anyone—he always lifts Soul into the greater stream of activity.

Through Its Chosen One does Sugmad administer Its will in creation. This plan was drawn up even prior to the unknown Living ECK Master who served before the coming of Polarian man.

The Living ECK Master takes under his wing those initiates who for some reason cannot reach their former Master in the other planes. But when he himself leaves the role as spiritual leader and passes the Rod of ECK Power to another, he no longer accepts new initiates—for this is contrary to the law of God.

ECK Masters generally run two missions at the same time—the main one headed by the Living ECK Master, and a microcosmic mission of personal interest that nevertheless ties in with the universal one and never interferes or detracts from it. All missions of Masters in all galaxies interlock with that of the Living ECK Master, like the cogs in the wheel of the ECK-Vidya.

History shows some Living ECK Masters in the past worked in public, while others were wholly unknown even to their near neighbors. Whatever their posture in the community, it depended upon the supreme command given them by the Sugmad at the moment they took on the Spiritual Mantle. Each messenger carries out his prescribed duties with single-minded devotion until his term is done.

Should a Master ever finish his mission and be reluctant to step aside for the next man, if such a thing were possible, the almighty power of Spirit would simply burn him to a crisp until he let go of the Rod of ECK Power. The spiritual leadership is always transferred at the instigation of the ECK!

One more thing that I would like to cover is the use of the orange light and the Blue Light for healing. The Audible Life Current is the total wave of Light and Sound, similar to white light before a prism breaks it down into beautiful colors. This rainbow of light can heal the physical and psychic bodies.

The orange light is for healing the physical body from disease, ailment, or accident. Go into contemplation and visualize yourself on the bed, surrounded by an orange stream of effervescent light waves. Direct the stream of orange light toward an injured or diseased organ—in your own body only. Never do this for another person unless you want his karma. Be aware that you may get indirect healing also, by obeying a sudden impulse to see a certain doctor.

The Blue Light also heals—but especially the Astral, Causal, and Mental bodies. In the same way as with the orange light, put attention upon this

I would like to cover the use of the orange light and the Blue Light for healing. The Audible Life Current is the total wave of Light and Sound, similar to white light before a prism breaks it down into beautiful colors. This rainbow of light can heal the physical and psychic bodies.

Blue Light during contemplation. Let its cleansing light wash over and around you for twenty minutes before dropping the exercise.

If you have a need for this, let this contemplative aid become part of your regular spiritual exercises for several weeks. It takes discipline to hold the inner channels open while the healing is to take place.

Experiment with these techniques until you find a tailor-made approach that fits you, for everyone is different.

32

WHO IS YOUR MASTER?

*O*n my 1981 trip to the South Pacific for a number of ECK leadership meetings, this question surfaced repeatedly since the passing of the Rod of ECK Power had occurred on October 22, 1981: "Who is now my Master?"

There is a great interest, and a natural one, about what is the Mahanta, and who is the Living ECK Master?

An ECKist who obtained a clear inner insight wrote in a letter: "The changeover in Masters was very difficult for me until I realized how wonderful it was! Unlike Christianity, I am not following a man. I am living a way of life and following a 'teaching'—not just one man."

The Spiritual Notebook points out that every Living ECK Master must go through the initiation of accepting the Rod of ECK Power. It is then that the ECK descends and enters into him, giving him the power of the Word of God. It has always been the ECK that is responsible for the presence of the Living Master upon this planet and in all the universes. Only the form of the ECK is changed as the

It has always been the ECK that is responsible for the presence of the Living Master upon this planet and in all the universes.

ECK power is handed down from one Master to his successor.

Another ECKist writes: "It is difficult to adjust to the reality of a new Living ECK Master . . . but it has brought home again the importance of the continuity and ongoing flow of the ECK in contrast to the personality of the Master."

As the present Living ECK Master, I represent the Sugmad as Its vehicle in the lower planes. You have the freedom to look for spiritual guidance and protection from whomever you wish, including Rebazar Tarzs, Peddar Zaskq, or myself.

The ECK is the ECK, no matter what body It uses to express Itself.

In 1965, there was a dramatic change in the Mahanta consciousness during the transition from Rebazar Tarzs to Peddar Zaskq. This present era of Mahantaship will continue two hundred to five hundred years, more or less, until the next greater change in the Mahanta Consciousness takes place.

During the current era, as always, whoever accepts the Rod of ECK Power becomes the Mahanta. Regardless of who the present Living ECK Master is, the Mahanta Consciousness continues to evolve as It derives from the pure, positive God Worlds, where creation continues.

The Mahanta is not a personality.

The greater change in the Mahanta Consciousness in 1965 had little to do with the personality of Paul Twitchell, who was merely the physical vehicle chosen by the ECK for the Mahantaship.

The Mahanta is a spiritual title that designates

Only the form of the ECK is changed as the ECK power is handed down from one Master to his successor. The ECK is the ECK, no matter what body It uses to express Itself.

the highest state of consciousness while still in this world and carrying on the duties of the Living ECK Master. Rebazar Tarzs, Fubbi Quantz, and Yaubl Sacabi have all passed through the state of Mahantaship and still retain it.

To find your own answer about who is your Master, read *The Shariyat-Ki-Sugmad*, Books One and Two, and also *The Spiritual Notebook*. Read a little bit about the Mahanta and the Rod of ECK Power, then, in contemplation, take your question within. If you are persistent and sincere, you will find the solution yourself and know the secret of who is your Master. It is not for anyone else to tell you.

The Mahanta is a spiritual title that designates the highest state of consciousness while still in this world and carrying on the duties of the Living ECK Master.

33
OUR NEW SPIRITUAL DIRECTION

A shift in spiritual direction is taking place. It is a transition from, What is the *form* of Eckankar? to, What is its *substance?* The future will see less of "This is who we are" and more of "This is what ECK principles are all about."

There will soon be a time when the world community will hear the name Eckankar and not have to ask, What is it? Our public classes will continue to expand from needing to explain "What is Eckankar?" to courses that deal with helpful spiritual insight, such as "This is how dreams work and why." ECK Arahatas will be sought out for what they teach, rather than for what group they come from.

The new consciousness is ready for ECK. The understanding of these new people outreaches the knowledge of their churches, and so they seek. When the form of illusion collides with the substance of truth, a fierce crosswind is born. These seekers huddle inside their caves of old beliefs, fearing the destruction that seems to play outside. The church feeds their emotions, but its doctrines are drained of Sound and Light. How can it then fulfill their spiritual yearning?

The future will see less of "This is who we are" and more of "This is what ECK principles are all about."

165

*Many from
this new
consciousness
will find the
love of ECK
because of
you, the
Arahata.*

Many from this new consciousness will find the love of ECK because of you, the Arahata. And many will stay on as members of their churches, to honor a duty to their families. It is these very people who one day will rise as a new order of ECK initiates. Paul Twitchell spoke of ECKists who would infiltrate the ranks of orthodox religions. This is what he meant.

In a dream, the Mahanta foretold the coming of this new spiritual generation to an ECK initiate. She saw a young man trying to get her attention. He wanted someone to notice his new sweater, but the weather was far too warm for such a heavy article of clothing. In the background stood a young woman, too preoccupied to notice him. So he began to converse with the dreamer, a mature woman. She complimented his good taste, and a line of friendship and communication opened between them. Soon he felt comfortable in shedding the heavy sweater.

The dreamer asked the Mahanta to help her understand this dream.

The young man is all the people of the world who are finding a new understanding or approach to life, but who also want help in understanding and adjusting to it. The heavy sweater is a symbol of their religious philosophy, which is out of season. The young woman represents the religions these people used to follow, but which no longer bring them satisfaction. The dreamer is an Arahata of the mature spiritual teachings of ECK. Her cordial manner of introducing ECK to newcomers gives them confidence to throw off past beliefs, which are now too heavy and uncomfortable.

This new age of spirituality might well be called "The Sharing of God." An ECK initiate recently came to this awareness. She was in a Satsang class which was studying the chapter in the first book of *The Shariyat* entitled "The Living ECK Master." In the HU chant at the start of class, she invited the Living ECK Master to attend. In her Spiritual Eye, she began to see cords of blue light connecting the six people in class that night. The cords formed a six-pointed blue star. Before opening her eyes, she asked the Inner Master what her contemplation meant.

The first thing that met her eyes when she reopened them was *The Shariyat* on her lap. The golden letters on its front now read, "The Sharing of God." She realized that *The Shariyat* is the sacred writing which the Master uses to tell people of the Sugmad.

Yet this experience shows even more than that. It shows that the ECK teachings must be given with love and not with fear. A very young child is often unwilling to part with its toy. Afraid to lose it, the child holds on tightly and screams, "Mine!" As he matures into a more complete person, he learns that sharing a toy does not necessarily mean he'll lose it. Eckankar is growing up. We are discovering better ways to share our knowledge of ECK with grace and love.

In a dream, an ECKist met an ECK Master who was fairly dark-skinned, perhaps a native of North Africa or the Near East. In an instant he vanished, but two music album covers appeared in his place, both showing a picture of the ECK Master from the waist up. The only difference was in the hats he wore. The hat on the left indicated music of a high spiritual nature; the right, enjoyable music—common ground, feet-on-the-earth material. Suddenly,

The golden letters on its front now read, "The Sharing of God." She realized that The Shariyat *is the sacred writing which the Master uses to tell people of the Sugmad.*

This is part of me: All the music, the art, the writings, and talks. All a way to tell people of the Sound and Light of ECK.

the two album covers came together and blended into one. The white light of ECK shot out; the album cover and the ECK Master were no longer seen.

Now the Mahanta spoke from the Light, "I am the Mahanta. This is part of me."

This is part of me: All the music, the art, the writings, and talks. All a way to tell people of the Sound and Light of ECK, and the Sugmad.

Stay or go?

CHAPTER TEN

Through Testing Times

34
STAY OR GO?

ome in ECK are like Coronado, the Spanish conquistador, who, from 1540 to 1542, tried to find the Indian kingdom of Gran Quivira. Legend held that its streets were paved with gold, and he wanted it because gold meant power. He and his soldiers crossed eastern Arizona, New Mexico, the Texas and Oklahoma panhandles, and went far into Kansas before turning back. Some ECK initiates make the same wandering journey off the direct path to God in search of power.

In this world we are in a precarious position, balanced midway between material and spiritual hungers. We find heaven to be a delicate state of consciousness that can be lost in a single moment of forgetfulness.

The chela's problem is his indecision as to how long he should stay by the Mahanta. He badly wants freedom, charity, and wisdom, but mostly, freedom. Freedom from any creed, religion, or teacher—and he wants that freedom now.

All throughout his time in ECK, he is beset by this question: When do I go on my own, Mahanta? At the very first initiation he must make the

We find heaven to be a delicate state of consciousness that can be lost in a single moment of forgetfulness.

decision: Stay or go? After all, *The Shariyat-Ki-Sugmad*, Book Two, says: "Once the decision is reached by the seeker to take the first step on the path of ECK, the disciple is no longer in need of the temporal, or the outer, instructions only, for he begins to acquire those which are spiritual, in relation to the unenlightened multitude." The first test for the neophyte is: Stay or go?

At the Second Initiation, the chela must make the decision again. This time three choices are before him: white magic, black magic, or the road of the purified Soul? More simply: Stay or go?

When the chela later becomes a new Mahdis, he is on trial for weeks or months as the false balance in him is replaced by the ECK. But if he fails the tests of Self-Realization, he could slip back into the mind worlds. He is a "dweller on the threshold," and the decision is again: Stay or go?

But the Kevalshar, initiate of the Eleventh Circle, knows his relationship with the Mahanta. *The Shariyat* says about him: "Rebirth is gained in this world which is the land of the Sugmad. . . . for the way to this rebirth in the Sugmad, a guide must be found. It is only the Mahanta, the Living ECK Master who can serve as the spiritual guide to lead the initiate into this world."

With this in mind, it is hard to see why ECK initiates still go off in pursuit of would-be masters who deal in psychic sensationalism. Even Higher Initiates are on a grand detour such as Coronado made to search for the fabled city of gold.

An ECK chela who dabbles in other teachings is like a fish that nibbles the bait on a fisherman's hook. The Kal keeps fresh bait in the water, but he catches only those who are naive about truth.

The first test for the neophyte is: Stay or go?

A few weeks ago an ECK chela attended a meeting by a master of a particular healing order. At the registration table, she was made to sign a pledge to complete the workshop, which included four initiations. To avoid a scene, she signed it. Later she asked the Living ECK Master if she had been wrong in attending the workshop but was assured she had not. When the pseudomaster had put pressure on her, she immediately asked the Mahanta inwardly for guidance. Upon reflection, it was obvious to her that the healer's four initiations were a sham. He taught the laying on of hands, which she knew was dangerous from her reading of the ECK discourses. In looking back at this experience, she saw that the healing energy of this teacher was only of the Kal.

Some ECK initiates are misusing ECK to heal the sick and are charging a fee for this service. This is wrong. They are taking on karma and will have to pay for it. The Kal government of the lower universes has authorized medical schools to teach students to become health practitioners. Licensed doctors, dentists, and other healers are granted relief from certain karma, since most of it is parceled out among the main body of healers. This safeguard is not available to someone who heals out of a misplaced sentiment of improving the lot of the downtrodden, but who has no idea of the karma behind the patient's condition.

Paul Twitchell spoke of the orange light. The orange light is only for one to heal himself, not others—especially not for a fee. This puts oneself before the ECK. People who abuse the practice of spiritual healing, whether by design or through ignorance, often do healings because of the influence it gives them over other people. In connection

Some ECK initiates are misusing ECK to heal the sick and are charging a fee for this service. This is wrong. They are taking on karma and will have to pay for it.

The safest healing is to tell the sick to see the best doctor available, and then have the patient write to the Mahanta, the Living ECK Master for the inner spiritual guidance in order to make a decision. This avoids all karma.

with this, pendulums and mediums are not part of spiritual healing in ECK either. The safest healing is to tell the sick to see the best doctor available, and then have the patient write to the Mahanta, the Living ECK Master for the inner spiritual guidance in order to make a decision. This avoids all karma.

An ECK chela who toys with psychic paths is subject to a psychic attack. One ECKist told of a psychic attack on him after a TV show that had a medium for a guest. The ECKist had submitted questions before the show, saying how some of the things said by the medium in an earlier interview sounded much like the ECK teachings. A couple of weeks later, a woman in black paid him a visit during contemplation. She asked to enter his state of consciousness, which he permitted because he was enamored of her. Immediately she began changing things around in him to suit herself, like a woman rearranging furniture in her host's living room. The medium had inwardly traced him to his home through his letter to the TV program. The ECK chela asked the Mahanta to get her out and restore his peace of mind.

Besides the cases mentioned above, other chelas, including some who consider themselves Higher Initiates, have been slipping off to see a medium on the West Coast who is controlled by an entity that makes predictions on future conditions and changes in the world. These individuals are poor examples as ECK leaders, because they do not believe ECK is the highest path to God. One must want God before everything else. The problem is that they want everything else before God.

An initiate who saw the situation above asked

why Higher Initiates would stoop to such nonsense. Why would longtime ECKists be caught by such sensationalism? She said, "I don't want to follow any more swamis, or Edgar Cayce readings, or Baba Ram Dasses." Only the Mahanta was important to her. She refused to let the Kal steal her away from the Sound and Light of God.

The agents of the Kal can trace the energy waves of an individual through a letter or a phone call, then they enter the chela's dream state and bother him. The Mahanta will sometimes not interfere in cases like this, because his words of caution have been ignored. Initiates who stray to psychic prophets still have more to learn about the Kal, and no amount of advice will do them any good, only hard experience. These individuals are actually looking for the path of power—and the Kal is raw power. The Mahanta will let them play with power until it brings them to their knees.

The disciple of the Mahanta is a person of charity. His strength is love, not power; therefore, he is among the strongest people on earth. He is like the owner of two Spanish swords, which have these respective inscriptions on them: "Do not draw me without reason," and "Do not sheathe me without honor." The disciple of the Mahanta is the humble man of God who does not seek trouble, but does defend his own in danger.

At the 1985 World Wide of ECK seminar in Atlanta, I quoted a profound observation by Paul Twitchell on power and the Kingdom of God. He said: "In a God-created universe, the secret of life is no power. When we come to the Kingdom of God, we find there is no power, only grace. It is by this grace that we survive in all universes, and no power

The disciple of the Mahanta is a person of charity. His strength is love, not power; therefore, he is among the strongest people on earth. He does not seek trouble, but does defend his own in danger.

of any kind can operate against us, in us, or through us. This puts us in a very humble position. As much as we may dislike it, we must acknowledge that we, of ourselves, do nothing."

Yet there will always be those who seek psychic knowledge from mediums in a vain search for power.

35
GETTING PAST
SPIRITUAL STAGNATION

year ago an initiate made the comment that he felt there really was such a thing as the holiday blues. It is a feeling of incompleteness and vague dread that the new year holds little promise over the old. The holiday blues and boredom are stepsisters. One negative state expresses the fear that there will be no growth in the future, while the latter reflects the spiritual stagnation of the moment. Both can be overcome by the creative techniques of ECK.

The Shariyat-Ki-Sugmad says that the three main parts of Eckankar are: the Spiritual Exercises of ECK, the constant presence of the Mahanta, and the chela doing all activities in the name of the Master. I cannot stress enough the importance of the spiritual exercises. The main difference between ECK and other religious teachings is that if the chela is faithful with the creative techniques, he can enter the kingdom of heaven while still in the physical body!

A devoted ECKist recently made a profound discovery about the reality of the ECK writings. The Inner Master took him to the inner planes

The Shariyat-Ki-Sugmad *says that the three main parts of Eckankar are: the Spiritual Exercises of ECK, the constant presence of the Mahanta, and the chela doing all activities in the name of the Master.*

179

where he was surprised to find the ECK writings more than mere allegories. "When I contemplated lately," he writes, "I would often begin to sense some room or structure in which I was doing so. I had often read that we go to the inner temple to worship, and so I decided to let the experience flow along. Over the last few months I have discovered a great structure in my contemplations. It reminds me of a soaring Gothic cathedral. Deep within is a small chapel-like area, and off this is a room like an inner sanctum to which the Light of the ECK shines very pure."

A vague or passing desire for God-Realization is not sufficient motivation. Too many people settle for psychic development and relief of ailments, both of which concern the human consciousness. The only thing worth Soul's struggle in the lower worlds is for It to return to the consciousness and joy of the God State. The key point so often ignored by the initiate is the admonition to seek ye first the kingdom of heaven and all things shall be added unto you.

The only thing worth Soul's struggle in the lower worlds is for It to return to the consciousness and joy of the God State.

Before the Spiritual Traveler allows anyone to unfold new powers, he insists that the individual first develop the neglected faculties. A Canadian citizen put her secret word to good use while manning a booth at a summer fair. With each silent chant, a person would soon approach the booth to ask about ECK or take an ECK book. "This happened often enough that I know now, by keeping my attention on the Inner Master and by chanting my secret word, I make possible the Master's linkup to certain Souls. What a great power and great discovery."

Soul spends entire cycles as an inhabitant in the worlds of matter, trying to regain communication with the Sugmad. Most religions teach their followers to use prayer—which is good—but prayer has had doubtful success in helping people reach God. How many churchmen know of the Light and Sound of ECK?

Neglect of the spiritual exercises brings an uncomfortable feeling of disorientation and lack of harmony to anyone who has ever tasted the sweet waters of life. In England, a chela began contemplation after a lengthy lapse in self-discipline. She found a quiet moment to reestablish communication with the Mahanta. "Something wonderful happened as though to reassure me," she said. "The Blue Star appeared and exploded into a dazzling white light which seemed to bathe me in love. . . . The guilt and unworthiness were swept away as this tremendous surge of love poured over me."

A number of years ago an ECKist was disturbed by occult predictions that the Pacific coast region of the United States would slip beneath the dark waters of the ocean, as did the mystical continent of Lemuria. With a nervous laugh, she asked the Living ECK Master, "Is there something we should know?" He just smiled and said, "You have my love." He was speaking as the ECK, the real substance behind the expression: "I am always with you."

People who have not yet surrendered their fears to the Light Giver misinterpret ECK-Vidya readings by the ECK Masters. Disaster can be averted in any given time frame—and often is! Initiates, as instruments for the ECK and as private individuals, bring balance to the sphere of their community.

"Love does not come to those who seek it, but to those who give love" read the golden words from *The Shariyat.* Thus life demands activity for inner growth.

Neglect of the spiritual exercises brings an uncomfortable feeling of disorientation and lack of harmony to anyone who has ever tasted the sweet waters of life.

The Inner Master makes his presence known in several ways. First comes the Light, then the Sound. Finally the Light body on the Astral Plane. At other times there comes a feeling of love.

A certain initiate, who had learned to let the cosmic current flow into him, did little to create an adequate outlet of service to ECK. "Until today I think I was looking at the question of receiving the next initiation as a test of my patience and humility. But it seems the test is more than one of simply waiting around for something to happen, but rather one of taking an active position and working to develop oneself."

The Inner Master makes his presence known in several ways. First comes the Light, then the Sound. Finally, the Master makes his appearance in the Nuri Sarup, the Light body on the Astral Plane. At other times there comes a feeling of love, like a warm cloak draped about the shoulders.

The greatest enlightenment for anyone is that all rulers of all planes are really the Mahanta, the Living ECK Master. The Mahanta is formless, says *The Shariyat*, in spite of having form. This insight comes on the Soul Plane at the court of Sat Nam. Henceforth the devotee sees the Light of ECK shining through the eyes of all whom he meets on the street. This is an astounding realization!

36
THROUGH TESTING TIMES

*L*et's retrace our route for a moment to see what conditions you can expect to contend with as initiates. *The Shariyat* speaks of the Vairagi Adepts of ECK as the Swordsmen of the Sugmad, for the spiritual path to God is hardly for the cowardly or the fainthearted.

A correspondent from a southern U.S. city defined her stand in relation to the ECK principles. She had become an initiate in 1971, prior to Paul Twitchell's translation, but for the next two years he still spoke to her through the inner channels. This lady is one of the rare persons who has made it easily through each change of ECK Mastership.

Every time the ECK rises to a new level of consciousness, as signaled by the passing of the Rod of ECK Power, a fallout occurs among the chelas. For one reason or another some cannot make the quantum leap to the higher state. The spent husks of spiritual failures dot the ditches along the road home. Their names fade from memory, and new people who find ECK in the future have never heard of them. A rugged proving ground is set up each time the ECK takes up another manifestation of Itself in a physical form.

The Shariyat speaks of the Vairagi Adepts of ECK as the Swordsmen of the Sugmad, for the spiritual path to God is hardly for the cowardly or the fainthearted.

Those who lightly turn their backs on the ECK will stray into the dust of the ages with a broken heart. Locked securely in their states of consciousness, they are repulsed by the Precepts of ECK and refuse to let go of the mind hooks that form their imperfect opinions and, worse, cut them off from the Audible Life Stream. The outcome is an estrangement from the spiritual community and is of their own doing. Thus, in turn, by their own efforts must they find the way back to the Sound Current. The ECK Masters are always nearby, but the outcasts find that the Third Eye is sealed shut against the rapture of God's essence, the ECK.

When the Swordsmen of the Sugmad walk among the nations of men there come pestilence, trial, heartache, broken homes, destruction in the earth, and the very heavens tremble for their glory. These are the messengers of God. Every initiate must know that he is making a deep commitment in his relationship with the Almighty, and that takes the utmost in courage. The Wilderness Road of the late eighteenth century, a dangerous trail blazed through the Cumberland Gap, is smooth sailing in comparison with the warfare that one encounters in his bid for *Moksha*, or liberation.

A favored belief has sprung up around the lives of the saviors who came to earth to bring light to the people of their times. The idea is that peace will surely reign in this cesspool of a world, and all will be well at the re-coming of a certain savior. The whole fabric of religion is woven from this wrong selection of facts that distorts the whole story of the purpose of creation. Earth is a training academy, not a botanical garden. Christ said things that are an embarrassment to today's theologians: "Think

Every initiate must know that he is making a deep commitment in his relationship with the Almighty, and that takes the utmost in courage.

not that I am come to send peace on earth: I came not to send peace, but a sword."

His role, in his own words, was "to set a man at variance against his father, and the daughter against her mother, and the daughter in law against her mother in law." Chaos likewise follows the ECK Adepts, for karma is speeded up wherever their footsteps pass.

The waves of the ECK Current come from an unexpected quarter to shake up the initiate who has fallen for the trap of the worship of personality. The outcome is foreseen, and the victim is like chaff blown from the wheat. He falls under the cloak of the Yama Dutas, the angels of darkness. The gains that he had carved out for himself are gone, while the spiritual currents slow down—then begin to spin in reverse order. The top of the world becomes a dreg heap. The retreat in awareness slips in by degrees, drying up his vitality like a river that boldly cuts a path into the desert in spring but is gone in the first heat of summer. One day Soul arouses Itself and finds Its bed on the cold, barren ground at the foot of the spiritual mountain, whose heights It had once roamed freely as a prince. Therefore, when an initiation in ECK is revoked, Soul has already done this to Itself on the inner planes.

How do the Masters of the Vairagi operate as Co-workers with God? Look at the hierarchy that works in this world. The holy scriptures of the Shariyat-Ki-Sugmad are hidden in two main locations: (1) The first main section is under the watchful eye of Fubbi Quantz in northern Tibet, and (2) the other part is kept in the Temple of Gare-Hira with Yaubl Sacabi. The third key figure in this triad

How do the Masters of the Vairagi operate as Co-workers with God? Look at the hierarchy that works in this world.

is the Tibetan, Rebazar Tarzs, who is the Torch-bearer of Eckankar. When the time comes for a new Living ECK Master to put on the Spiritual Mantle, the successor is chosen from among the band of ECK Adepts. He has already made his way to the high regions of God after going through all these levels: the acolyte, the initiate, the Mahdis, and the Adept—where he joins the ECK community of Masters.

The Sugmad alone gives the initiation of the passing of the Rod of ECK Power.

In *The Spiritual Notebook* Paul Twitchell says of a new ECK Master: "His turn will come to be the Living ECK Master, should it be so established among the hierarchy of the Vairagi Order."

The Sugmad alone gives the initiation of the passing of the Rod of ECK Power. The hierarchy carries out its role in making plans for the transition from one Master to another. The hierarchy, reflecting the will of the Sugmad, makes the decision as to who is the most qualified being within the order to become the Sat Guru, the leader of Eckankar. The Living ECK Master, or sometimes an appointed Master, does the final phase of training, but all the Masters have a close interest in the candidate's spiritual education. Rebazar Tarzs then passes the Rod of ECK Power to the new Godman at midnight on October 22 if the retiring Living ECK Master is no longer in the physical body.

All of these ECK Masters play their parts as Co-workers with God, for the entire ritual is under the guidance of the Sugmad and has ever been since before the dawn of time.

According to *The Shariyat,* when one "renounces attachments while remaining balanced evenly in spiritual and worldly successes and failures, then he has been liberated."

CHAPTER ELEVEN

Success in ECK

37

BRUSHING YOUR
OBSTACLES ASIDE

several times during my lecture tour in the
South Pacific countries in late 1982, people
said that emphasis on the unit of Soul
made ECKists look selfish to them. All the while I
had been pointing out a very important thing. We
must give back some kind of service to all life in
thanks for the shower of Light and Sound that goes
with spiritual unfoldment. Soul lives forever by giving, not by receiving. First, however, we must be
able to help ourselves before we are of any use to
our fellowman.

This brings up the elements needed for anyone
to gain in spirituality. One must first find the
Living ECK Master, who can link him up with the
great Sound Wave. This leads to the kingdom of
heaven in this lifetime or the next. What trips up
Soul in achieving this worthy goal? Simply procrastination! In several cities on the tour, ECK leaders
arrived half an hour late for vital meetings. They
did not recognize the important self-discipline of
being on time.

Talons of Time, the spiritual adventure novel
written by Paul Twitchell, tells of the Time Makers'

*We must give
back some
kind of service
to all life in
thanks for the
shower of
Light and
Sound that
goes with
spiritual
unfoldment.
Soul lives
forever by
giving, not by
receiving.*

191

attempts to manipulate the strings of attachment in order to keep Soul bound to the human state of consciousness. One of the strings is procrastination. For this reason, in ECK leadership, the ECK Masters underline the value of setting goals and seeing each cycle through to completion.

There are three elements to the state of beingness that relate to setting goals: (1) The starting point (where you are at rest), (2) the passage or transition from the starting point to the goal, and (3) the goal (where you are again at rest). What does all this mean? Only this: the Negative Power tries to trap Soul by introverting It during the transition or passage between the starting point and goal. Maybe this seems too complicated but this introversion shows up as procrastination, which keeps the chela away from the spiritual exercises.

One humorous conversation on the South Pacific tour involved the fellow who complained about a lack of spiritual success. When asked if he did the spiritual exercises, he said, "Yes, I do them regularly." Further questioning revealed that "regularly" to him did not mean "daily," but only "every so often." No wonder he was not having any success. Putting off the Spiritual Exercises of ECK will stunt spiritual growth.

Attachment, one of the most insidious of the five passions, is the mother of procrastination. We set undue store by our business affairs, or involvement with the family and associates, so that we lose track of our spiritual interests.

Meditation also leads to spiritual introversion. That is why the Vairagi ECK Masters recommend contemplation instead: "Go inside and do something!"

Attachment throws up seemingly insurmount-

In ECK leadership, the ECK Masters underline the value of setting goals and seeing each cycle through to completion.

able obstacles on the narrow path to God. An ECKist, who wished to go to a Light and Sound meeting in Boston in November of 1982, faced several good reasons that could have blocked his attempts to go there. First of all, he felt he could not afford it because his cash was tied up in building a new home. Secondly, he feared his wife would object strongly, and, finally, he was sure that his boss would never let him off work on Saturday.

In contemplation, he asked the "little blue dot of Light" for help in getting to Boston. That night when he talked to his wife, she said without any hesitation, "That would be great! We could get my mother to watch the baby and have a chance to see a new city." The next day he told his boss, "I need Saturday off." (This was a day after the boss had lectured him about having to work on weekends.) His employer just looked up at him and said, "OK, have a nice time." The next day came a refund for a bill the ECKist had double paid eight months earlier. So the couple went to Boston, all obstacles brushed neatly aside by Spirit. The ECKist had trusted the little blue dot of Light, which was the Inner Master.

Problems befall anyone who slips in his disciplines and stops the Spiritual Exercises of ECK. Having lost the true inner guidance, he resorts to power politics in order to carry out his local duties. The initiate who turns to power to get his own way has a broken communication line between himself and Divine Spirit. There is always a way to work together in harmony while giving out the ECK doctrines. When the Living ECK Master sees this broken contact with Spirit, he steps quietly into the background and will not say anything for weeks,

There is always a way to work together in harmony while giving out the ECK doctrines.

perhaps, hoping that the sharp lessons of life will reopen the eyes of the spiritually blind.

Man must not become so bound up with duties or worldly interests that he forgets how one day he must leave them all behind when he drops the body forever. The virtue that overcomes attachment is vairag, or detachment. According to *The Shariyat*, when one "renounces attachments while remaining balanced evenly in spiritual and worldly successes and failures, then he has been liberated."

The virtue that overcomes attachment is vairag, or detachment.

38
INSIGHT FROM THE ESSENCE OF GOD

*T*his month I want to discuss spiritual strength. Hardly ever do I mention the Kal Niranjan, because this entity is well known in religious history, as well as in the ECK works. After we accept its role in the divine plan as an educator, we quit futile efforts to resist it.

The ECK Masters seldom harp upon a seeker's faults when opening the individual's Spiritual Eye. Instead, they stress the opposite virtues.

A chela disclosed that he had met the Mahanta during morning contemplation. A question he wished to ask was this: "How did you conquer the Kal force?" Even while writing this question down on paper he knew there was no pat answer, for all answers already lie in the awareness of Soul. The challenge: "How to focus and bring the answers into practice?"

"I have a lot of trouble with this negative force," he continued, "and I wonder over and over: Why did the Sugmad have to create this negative side of Itself? I know the answer. I just wonder if it's all really necessary."

The ECK Masters seldom harp upon a seeker's faults when opening the individual's Spiritual Eye. Instead, they stress the opposite virtues.

First of all, obstacles give Soul strength to rise above the pull of the material worlds. When It finally enters the regions of the Nameless One—Advaita—Soul tastes the magnificence and splendor of the Sugmad in all Its glory.

Opposition and problems are a part of life. They compel the traveler to develop randomity and common sense along the footpath to spiritual liberation. The ECKist looks at things as a whole, while the uninitiated locks everything into logical categories. The strength of the chela, maintains *The Shariyat-Ki-Sugmad*, is that he "is able to face every problem in life and bring about his own solution to it without having to depend on another."

Gravity presses the baby down in its crib at birth. Yet the baby slowly gathers strength until one day it can lift its tiny head in defiance of gravity. Spiritual strength comes in like manner. Handling ever greater obstacles thrown up by the Negative Power, Soul is lifted above the theater of despair and failure. Every imaginable barrier arises to delay the ECKist on the road home to God.

The Law of Growth in the lower worlds demands that everything must go slower and slower as it ages. Finally one settles into a rut, becomes less mobile, until death is the final state. Only the Spiritual Exercises of ECK can renew consciousness and insure Soul an escape from rebirth and death.

We sidestep misfortune and trouble whenever possible but are ever instrumental in easing the suffering of the helpless.

A hospital worker was assigned to a patient recovering from a serious operation that left blinding pain, and the patient's immense agony created turmoil in the chela herself. Right away she chanted her secret word. This opened the gates of consciousness so that Spirit could bring healing into the recovery room. The ECK quickly soothed the patient's torment through miraculous means. This ECKist knows to call upon the Mahanta rather than trying to heal the sick herself, which only causes bad karma through ignorance of the spiritual laws.

If you have tried without success to be rid of an obstacle, release it to Spirit. But how? The Snowball technique works well, and other methods are listed in the ECK books. Go back to the basics!

Even the Living ECK Master gets help to complete his mission. Although spiritual succor comes straight from the Sugmad, the Council of Nine offers direct assistance when opposition halts the distribution of Eckankar in the lower worlds.

What does living ECK mean for you? The spiritual exercises open a direct line to the ECK. The secret word expands the consciousness so that we can grasp solutions already at hand. Once you catch the knack of getting insight from the Essence of God, then you are free to examine and study everything in life to your heart's content.

These two points are proposed to give you strength in all your struggles with life: First, place the image of the Mahanta, the Living ECK Master in the Tisra Til. Then look to that ideal for spiritual aid. Second, find an activity you really like to do. Take up a hobby or pastime that gives you a strong outflow of the Audible Life Current.

The spiritual exercises open a direct line to the ECK. The secret word expands the consciousness so that we can grasp solutions already at hand.

39
FINDING SUCCESS IN ECK

What kind of person will find success in ECK? First, he has an underlying sense of order, because the creations of ECK have order. Second, he loves beauty for its own sake, for behind the trials of living are justice and beauty. Third, he has a sense of wonder. The ECK continually unfolds new patterns of life that catch us by surprise, keeping us alert and conscious of the Sugmad.

These three elements appear in every aspect of a true seeker's life. In time, they even shape his dreams. Day and night dreams change from poorly sketched, broken, or senseless ones to creations of wonder, order, and beauty. The difference is not in his dreams, but in how he sees them. As he unfolds spiritually, he becomes more and more aware of the silver lining in every experience of life. He finds a deeper understanding of ECK. And eventually, this shows in all his dreams.

Some chelas give up too soon on the spiritual path of ECK. Their defeat usually comes from a lack of self-discipline. They come close to the secrets of ECK, but they let their thoughts and beliefs scatter like seeds before the wind. Real self-discipline

Some chelas give up too soon on the spiritual path of ECK. Their defeat usually comes from a lack of self-discipline. Real self-discipline centers on the Spiritual Exercises of ECK.

centers on the Spiritual Exercises of ECK. It always has, and it always will.

Nineteen ninety-one is the Year of the Vahana. RESAs will set up Vahana (missionary) teams in their regions over the coming weeks and months. Each team has three to nine people who like to carry the teachings of ECK into the world and have a special talent for it. They will need your help. If your team needs someone to give a talk or help in some other way with the Vahana program, please offer your service. Talents such as speaker, writer, scheduler, or any other skill can help people find the Light and Sound of God.

The two topics above—the self-discipline of spiritual exercises and the Vahana effort—lead into the following story. This story shows how a closed mind, composed of fears, causes all kinds of problems.

An ECK couple needed to be out of town for several days to attend a seminar. They asked a stable woman of about forty to stay in their home and care for their three children. They had known her for two years: She was the perfect sitter.

The first night when the parents called home, the sitter said their seven-year-old daughter had a fever and refused to sleep in her room. The next night, conditions had deteriorated further. This same child, said the sitter, now had a fear of her dolls. The girl had told a complete stranger (who later turned out to be the sitter's minister) about everything she feared in the home. This fear included pictures of the ECK Masters in the parents' bedroom, where the sitter slept.

The inner voice of the Mahanta told the mother to return home immediately. She arrived at 1:30 a.m. and found all three children at the front door,

wide awake. She asked them what had happened
during her absence from home. The first night, the
children overheard the sitter crying on the phone.
She told the other party she couldn't sleep because
of the ECK pictures in the bedroom. The sitter,
awake the whole night, kept the lights on and TV
blaring.

The next day, the sitter took the ECK couple's
seven-year-old daughter to her minister to pray
over the child. The minister spoke in tongues, trying to convince the girl to "accept Jesus." Worse, the
sitter told the ECK children that their religion was
a cult.

*This woman
had violated
the spiritual
space of the
children by
pressing her
beliefs upon
them.*

This woman had violated the spiritual space of
the children by pressing her beliefs upon them.
After the mother heard the story, she said she was
taking the children with her (to the ECK seminar
in Orlando). The sitter and her child could stay
overnight if they wished, but they were to leave in
the morning. Five minutes later, the sitter was out
the door. Her fear was so strong that she didn't even
bother to change out of her nightgown.

The ECK family immediately did a HU chant.
The seven-year-old girl pictured a river and a basket. She put the minister's strange words into the
basket and let them drift out of sight down the
river.

The mother has a thirty-year background with
that fundamental church group. That religion had
once also instilled in her an irrational fear of the
unknown. This story is not an indictment against
this religion, but against fear and ignorance. People
like that believe it is OK to impose their beliefs (and
fears) upon others.

What was the outcome of all this? The ECK

husband said that the sitter had committed a serious violation of the spiritual law. He predicted it would have consequences for her. His words were prophetic. Four days later the mother called the sitter, who answered the phone in tears. The baby-sitting experience was still affecting the woman. The mother said that although the sitter had done what appeared right, one does not interfere in others' spiritual space. Especially when it involves their children. The sitter's fear, the ECK mother further explained, was from a lack of understanding. It was certainly not from any real threat. By the end of the phone call, the sitter had stopped crying. The next day, however, she packed up and moved out of state.

Sadly, the sitter's religion had left her completely unprepared to face the simplest realities of life. On the other hand, the mother said that since this experience, her family appreciates more than ever the freedom they have found in ECK.

Is it any wonder that this is the Year of the Vahana? It is time to tell people about the Light and Sound, and about God's love. Help your Vahana team in whatever way you can.

It is time to tell people about the Light and Sound, and about God's love.

Another way to God-Realization is to give loving care
and attention to everything you do, because of your love
for Sugmad.

CHAPTER TWELVE

Going Home to God

40
SOUL'S UNIQUENESS

*I*nitiates in all circles of ECK need a reminder that they are truly Soul, which is
a unique reflection of God, or the Sugmad.
A characteristic of Soul is Its individuality. This
means that the spiritual experiences of one person
may or may not be like those of another. It all depends upon the line of unfoldment that any particular Soul chooses to follow in Its spiritual evolution
to become a God-Realized being.

Some ECK initiates are distressed to find they
do not have the glamorous Soul Travel adventures
described by others. Therefore, they wrongly feel
they are missing the heart of whatever ECK is all
about. Soul Travel is a means for Soul to extend Its
awareness from the human to the spiritual state of
consciousness. It is a particular approach to an
individual's expansion of awareness. But there is
more than one way to reach the vantage point of
God Consciousness.

The teachings of ECK are not to make anyone
feel that he is a failure if he is not conscious of Soul
Travel. A person may try to do the spiritual exercises on a regular schedule but become upset

*Initiates in all
circles of ECK
need a
reminder that
they are truly
Soul, which is
a unique
reflection of
God, or the
Sugmad.*

because nothing happens. He may blame himself for any shortcoming, not wishing to fault the ECK teachings. But is it necessary to carry the feelings of guilt from our pre-ECK instruction into Satsang? There is no guilt involved, nor should anyone be made to feel less than another in a Satsang class because he has had no experiences in Soul Travel, or in the Light and Sound of God. All these experiences come to one when the inner preparations have been made, and not until then.

What chance do I have to reach God-Realization when I don't Soul Travel? is a valid question. But look beyond Soul Travel.

Look also beyond having an inner experience in an ECK Satsang class. An initiate and her husband, both High Initiates, went to a class on *The Precepts of ECKANKAR*. There were fourteen other initiates in class. The Arahata asked the class members to choose a paragraph from the second discourse and to contemplate upon it. After contemplation, the other fourteen told of beautiful experiences, but the two visitors had nothing at all to talk about. So they felt left out, as if they really did not belong to the ECK group.

To allow each individual in class his beingness, the Arahata can ask the class members whether they would like to share certain experiences during a five- or ten-minute segment of class called "Spotlight on ECK." The experiences recounted in this portion of the class can include insights of the chela since the last meeting. They need not be limited to just the experiences of any in-class contemplation. The Arahata can choose volunteers from the class at random, instead of going around the room in order. Nor will it be likely that everyone can tell his

To allow each individual in class his beingness, the Arahata can ask the class members whether they would like to share certain experiences during a five- or ten-minute segment of class called "Spotlight on ECK."

inner experiences during the short "Spotlight" section of class.

This is not to say that personal experiences are to be given only in the "Spotlight on ECK" portion of class. That will however be a special time for the chelas to enjoy stories (if there even are any) of others who have a growing awareness of ECK in their lives. The idea is not to cause embarrassment to people because their experiences and insights are not gained directly through Soul Travel, or the Sound and Light of God. Insights into the spiritual reason for happenings in everyday life are often more revealing of the ways that the Holy Spirit uses to lift each of us to be better spiritual creatures.

After I wrote to an initiate in New York about putting Soul Travel into perspective, he replied: "What you said in the letter about being aware of doing Soul Travel, or of the Light and Sound—I have considered and have decided to just try and live ECK rather than seeking pictures in the Third Eye. If and when awareness comes—good. Until then, I'll keep trying to be a channel in whatever way I can." This is living in ECK without the need for labels.

The Mahanta, the Living ECK Master has a purpose in giving a certain experience to one, but not to another. All have their particular groundings in ECK, and he works within the conscious development of the individual.

You do not have to Soul Travel to be successful in ECK. Another way to God-Realization is to give loving care and attention to everything you do, because of your love for Sugmad.

I am going step-by-step with the whole movement of ECK. First, attention is on Soul Travel;

Insights into the spiritual reason for happenings in everyday life are often more revealing of the ways that the Holy Spirit uses to lift each of us to be better spiritual creatures.

Give your love to God, the Holy Spirit, and to the Mahanta— and your spiritual house will always be in order.

then, more on the Light and Sound; finally, on the love of service to God for Its sake alone. Some ECKists, during this evolution that will occur over the next few years, will be drawn to Soul Travel, others to Light and Sound, and still others to service to God. Each of these three elements is an equally important part in the outer message of ECK as it develops in the future.

Give your love to God, the Holy Spirit, and to the Mahanta—and your spiritual house will always be in order. ❀

41
How to Be the HU

From time to time it's necessary to speak to you about the Friday fast. What is it? What is the proper way to do it? Why do it at all?

In the early days of Eckankar, we used to practice one of three Friday fasts: (1) a water fast for twenty-four hours; (2) a partial fast of fruit, fruit juice, or only one meal for the entire day; or (3) a mental fast. The recommended fast for today is the mental fast. The other two can be harmful to persons with certain health conditions. The mental fast does not need the approval of a physician, and it is the safest and most convenient for anyone to use for spiritual growth.

The path of ECK is the middle path. As such, one need not indulge in excesses of any kind to gain spiritually—and this includes the stress of food fasts.

Here are a few points about fasting in general. The water fast may appeal to people who in past lives liked to wear hair shirts as a sign of their love for God. Of course, God does not go in for such odd behavior to express one's love, and the practice of depriving oneself of food often eroded into an act of

The path of ECK is the middle path. As such, one need not indulge in excesses of any kind to gain spiritually— and this includes the stress of food fasts.

vanity. The person who could fast longer than others felt it to be a mark of superiority. But Sugmad has no use for such human pride.

The fruit or fruit-juice fast can harm a diabetic, of course. If I were to insist that an initiate keep that fast—and he couldn't due to medical reasons—would it be right to limit his spiritual growth in such a manner?

But there is the Friday mental fast.

The mental fast is both easy and difficult, much harder than the water or partial fast if done correctly. It means keeping your attention upon the Mahanta all day long on Friday.

There are several ways to do it.

There are several ways to do the mental fast.

One way is to sing HU inwardly or outwardly. Another way to do the mental fast is to chant your secret word. A third way is to do everything that day in the name of the Mahanta. You may also keep your attention on him, whether or not you're doing anything at all. But why fast on Friday?

You've heard me say repeatedly that truth builds upon truth. Thus, it may also be that a new spiritual path borrows practices from old religions, updates them, and thus they become an integral part of the new religion. That is what happened to Christianity. It did borrow and alter holidays and ceremonies from pagan religions. In Eckankar, and in every other path to God, there is the same regard for what uplifts people spiritually in older paths.

For a while, Paul Twitchell was a Catholic. He saw the value of Friday as a day of special reverence for God, so later he used that day as the basis for the Friday fast in Eckankar. The Catholic Church lost something of deep value when it began to downplay its day of fasting. It actually lost the heart of its self-discipline.

It will startle some people in Eckankar to think that our fast day is fashioned after that once-familiar day in the Catholic Church. Here again, it takes a spiritual overview to see truth. Where do you think the Catholic Church got the idea? From ECK.

All religions spring from the ECK. Look closely at a religious practice before dismissing it as a superstitious rite. Why let *your* vanity and ignorance show?

The ECK has made all religions. Each path fulfills the inner needs of Souls at a given place in their rise to spiritual freedom.

So what does a special day of fasting do?

It helps you develop the inner discipline to reach God-Realization. You learn the habit of being in ECK. Every moment. Every day.

Then, when at the bedside of a loved one in critical health, you will remember to sing HU as a way of saying, "I love you." If you are a student in a difficult class on cooking, nursing, or computer science, you will remember to look upon the class instructor as the agent through whom the Mahanta is working. Or should you live in a community where people of a fundamentalist religion shun you, you will remember to call upon the Mahanta. He is always there with the Light and Sound of God to bring you joy.

Yes, the Friday fast is very important for you spiritually. In time, you will find it more easy and natural than ever to be in a high state of being every moment of your life.

Then you will be the HU.

The ECK has made all religions. Each path fulfills the inner needs of Souls at a given place in their rise to spiritual freedom.

42
THE LONG ROAD
TO GOD CONSCIOUSNESS

*T*hese are thoughts about the usually long road to God Consciousness. It is a long road for a reason. The few who want the God State right now could not handle it. What it is they want, they don't know. But their pride says, "Buck away, little bronco! This buckaroo can ride anything on four legs." Only, the God State is not something on four legs, and it's not a three-minute ride, but goes on and on and on.

People are in an unconscious state most of the time, even while awake. They are in the habit of blaming others for what goes wrong with them-selves. They haven't the pluck to take their own lives by the horns and make themselves happy— yet they feel ready to claim the God State. That would be as if Soul made the evolutionary jump straight from bug to man and then expected to excel in human society.

If one were to leap from unconsciousness to total awareness in one bound, it would be a quick rebound to the unconscious state. The shock of the God State would put him in a home for the mentally distressed.

The few who want the God State right now could not handle it. What it is they want, they don't know.

In *The Spiritual Notebook*, Paul Twitchell says, "We can move into this state of God Consciousness, but to stay there we must learn to retain our full awareness of it while continuing to carry out the daily affairs of life."

Therefore, in ECK, the steps to the kingdom of heaven are in this order: (1) coming into the awakened awareness of the physical state, then (2) arriving at a partial awareness of the physical and inner states, and finally (3) having full consciousness in both the physical and inner states at all times, which is a condition not easily reconciled.

One in the God State no longer sees the things of life in his accustomed ways of old. For now the mischief of certain people on the inner and outer planes is revealed to him. Some of them would even harm him. So it is a matter of forever being on guard.

The God-Conscious person IS the ECK.

The God-Conscious person IS the ECK. It is up to him to watch out for himself. He has to be aware every moment that total awareness is always at hand. He is in a state of readiness in all worlds, every minute, for it is a matter of survival.

Some people in ECK celebrate themselves, imagining they have the genius to go from the First to the Twelfth Initiation without delay. Yet they cannot last a week without cheating someone, telling gossip, starting a needless argument, giving their word and breaking it, and bungling their lives in too many ways to mention. Naively, they suppose that God Consciousness can change them into something they're not, like a pumpkin turning into a carriage, Cinderella becoming a princess, or a frog being restored as a prince.

But these people don't even love God.

The God State means to love the Sugmad, to be in total agreement with It, to trust It to guide us into the areas of life where we may use our creative talents for the good of all. But if given a chance to serve ECK in a humble capacity, these people first evaluate the working conditions, the career path, the benefits, the working hours, and whether the supervisor will be man or woman. Such people do not qualify for God Consciousness.

Living in ECK means having a love so filling that any dimension of service is gratefully given to God. Those who give generous service to the Sugmad receive the richest of gifts, without the need for asking.

Living in ECK means having a love so filling that any dimension of service is gratefully given to God.

I see and know things today that would have crushed me as a Second Initiate, or even as a Fifth. The willful acts of self-important chelas are a minor part of my concerns. My work is mainly in the other worlds, simply because there are so many Souls in them.

Many people on earth are quite satisfied to flounder in the wretchedness of body, mind, and spirit. It is because they do not know anything else. Give a blessing to someone in the human consciousness, and he will pick it apart to determine what you really meant by it. Give a furnished new home to a family whose karma has set them in a big-city ghetto, and in no time the property will likely be in ruins. This reflects the low state of consciousness that some never wish to leave. They are happy to endure and support anything the hand of karma furnishes them.

Happily, 95 percent of the ECK initiates are truly aspiring for the God realm. For them, the pursuit of God-Realization is everything.

In this respect I would mention dream travel. When people interpret their dreams, they should be kind to themselves. The dream should be seen with them in the hero position. Everything in the dream is to foster and preserve the good estate of the dreamer. In ECK a dream works on the principle of self-preservation and will tell the dreamer exactly what to do for survival. He will be shown the problem and its solution. If he interprets his dreams from a standpoint of survival, he knows that everything will work out for his good.

This is what it means to trust the ECK, to surrender to the Mahanta. Every dream experience will work out right if the dreamer will go through it in readiness, ever on the alert. This is a desirable mode for interpreting dreams.

The perspective on God Consciousness and the dreamer was needed in this Wisdom Note.

Every dream experience will work out right if the dreamer will go through it in readiness, ever on the alert.

43
GOING HOME TO GOD

*T*he first spiritual teachings that man saw in the modern historical era arose from India. This old land, in turn, had its wise men learning the tenets of wisdom at the feet of the ECK Masters of Atlantis. These ancient spiritual travelers included such stalwarts as Decates, Castrog, and Supaku.

India became heir apparent to the arcane knowledge once centered in Atlantis before its destruction by fire and water as correctly prophesied by Castrog. The king-priests, called the Tat Tsoks because of their worship of the supreme Deity known as Tat, ignored Castrog's warnings about the dangers of black magic. They unwittingly disturbed the natural magnetic forces of the land and doomed it to a grave beneath the dark ocean waters.

The old men of India passed the light of ECK knowledge to new nations that formed after the third worldwide cataclysm of earthquakes and volcanoes that broke up the islands and continents that had been Atlantis. The Egyptians, fond of the mysteries, developed the cult of Isis and Osiris, as well as a simplified but jumbled understanding of

The first spiritual teachings that man saw in the modern historical era arose from India. This old land, in turn, had its wise men learning the tenets of wisdom at the feet of the ECK Masters of Atlantis.

the ECK force that they personified in Horus, the sky god.

The Greeks, mere children to both the Hindus and Egyptians in the gathering of the secret laws, learned of the dim history of lost Atlantis only after Solon, Greek patriarch and lawgiver, made a visit to the Egyptian wise men as late as the sixth century BC.

The ECK Stream of consciousness sweeps down through layers of cosmic regions and worlds until Its perpetual message is brought to people on Earth by Its chief agent, the Mahanta, the Living ECK Master. The world is never without him, for the line of ECK Adepts originated before the first Aryan people were placed here by colonists from Jupiter.

The Mahanta appears with renewed splendor in every yuga and walks among people today.

The Mahanta appears with renewed splendor in every yuga and walks among people today. The knowledge and wisdom afforded him is far in advance of the doctrines peddled by popular religion, for his mission is to teach the techniques of Soul Travel. These simple exercises are a proven method for Soul to start Its homeward journey to God.

The Vairagi Masters keep away from the cumbersome systems of theology devised by the black-robed clergy. The intention of the spiritual hierarchy is to demonstrate to an individual the hearing and seeing powers of Soul through the spiritual exercises.

A unique organ of sight for Soul is the Tisra Til, the Third Eye. This is the Spiritual Eye, the seat of Soul in the human body. Its physical counterpart is the pineal body, which is located directly between and behind the eyebrows—almost at the direct center of the brain.

Descartes, the French mathematician and phi-

losopher of the seventeenth century, believed the
pineal body to be the seat of the "self," but science
dismisses it as a near-useless museum piece left
over from the primitive vertebrates.

Nevertheless the ECK Masters call this the
Tenth Door. The other nine body openings all lead
out to the external world, but the Spiritual Eye is
a principal gateway in man that opens to the inter-
nal worlds, the heavens of God. Detection of it is the
discovery of the way station that Soul uses to boost
Itself into the unutterably magnificent regions of
Light and Sound above Sach Khand that defy description.

"Sit down," says the primordial Mahanta. "Sit
down and shut your eyes. Gaze sweetly into the
Spiritual Eye and sing softly a name of God, such
as HU, Sugmad, or Akaha. Give twenty minutes or
half an hour to this drill each day, for only then can
I show you the face of the Absolute, which you call
God."

The simple teaching of Eckankar is this: how to
contact the Light and Sound of God, which have the
power to give spiritual liberation in this lifetime. A
devotee was to investigate his path through contemplation, study, and service, advised Paul Twitchell,
for how else could he tell whether this was the au-
thentic knowledge of God or not?

Why do the many paths to God compete with
each other to lure innocent people away from their
beliefs? A person's temple of consciousness is holy
indeed, for each individual must make his own way
to the Sugmad without falling victim to clever mar-
keting tricks. Soul must assume Its rightful position as a creator in the endless span of creation and
be a Co-worker with God.

The simple teaching of Eckankar is this: how to contact the Light and Sound of God, which have the power to give spiritual liberation in this lifetime.

The seeds of Truth are flung throughout all corners of the continents, countries, and islands of the four grand divisions. Nothing is withheld from anybody who has earned the right to them. His Spiritual Eye is opened by careful degrees so that the black-and-white worlds of karma appear to him in living color. The initiate of the Second Circle starts to understand the underlying play behind the dominion of tyrants, politicians, and priests.

The observance of truth comes a bit at a time. Meanwhile the Mahanta, the Living ECK Master and the ECK Adepts stand like silent sentinels in the background, watching for the initiate's reaction to the preliminary tests in Eckankar. Will he stay or will he go? As he passes one, another is put before him. He must take each bit of truth with a pure, loving heart and more will be given to him.

The ancient truth still rings today, with freshness instilled by the enormous, incomprehensible energy of the ECK Life Stream—which is nothing other than illimitable love.

The ancient truth still rings today, with freshness instilled by the enormous, incomprehensible energy of the ECK Life Stream—which is nothing other than illimitable love. The Tenth Door is being opened wider for you who love the Sugmad with all your heart and being.

I am always with you.

GLOSSARY

Words set in SMALL CAPS are defined elsewhere in this glossary.

ARAHATA. *ah-rah-HAH-tah* An experienced and qualified teacher of ECKANKAR classes.

BLUE LIGHT. How the MAHANTA often appears in the inner worlds to the CHELA or seeker.

CHELA. *CHEE-lah* A spiritual student.

ECK. *EHK* The Life Force, the Holy Spirit, or Audible Life Current which sustains all life.

ECKANKAR. *EHK-ahn-kahr* Religion of the Light and Sound of God. Also known as the Ancient Science of SOUL TRAVEL. A truly spiritual religion for the individual in modern times. The teachings provide a framework for anyone to explore their own spiritual experiences. Established by PAUL TWITCHELL, the modern-day founder, in 1965. The word means "Co-worker with God."

ECK MASTER(S). Spiritual Masters who can assist and protect people in their spiritual studies and travels. The ECK Masters are from a long line of God-Realized SOULS who know the responsibility that goes with spiritual freedom.

GOD-REALIZATION. The state of God Consciousness. Complete and conscious awareness of God.

HU. *HYOO* The most ancient, secret name for God. The singing of the word *HU* is considered a love song to God. It can be sung aloud or silently to oneself.

INITIATION. Earned by a member of ECKANKAR through spiritual unfoldment and service to God. The initiation is a private ceremony in which the individual is linked to the Sound and Light of God.

KAL NIRANJAN, THE. *KAL nee-RAHN-jahn* The Kal; the negative power, also known as Satan or the devil.

KLEMP, HAROLD. The present MAHANTA, the LIVING ECK MASTER. SRI Harold Klemp became the Mahanta, the Living ECK Master in 1981. The spiritual name of Sri Harold Klemp is WAH Z.

LIVING ECK MASTER. The title of the spiritual leader of ECKANKAR. His duty is to lead SOUL back to God. The Living ECK Master can assist spiritual students physically as the Outer Master, in the dream state as the Dream Master, and in the spiritual worlds as the Inner Master.

MAHANTA. *mah-HAHN-tah* A title to describe the highest state of God Consciousness on earth, often embodied in the LIVING ECK MASTER. He is the Living Word. An expression of the Spirit of God that is always with you.

MAHDIS. *MAH-dees* The initiate of the Fifth Circle (SOUL PLANE); often used as a generic term for all High Initiates in ECK.

PEDDAR ZASKQ. *PEH-dahr ZASK* The spiritual name for PAUL TWITCHELL, the modern-day founder of ECKANKAR, and the MAHANTA, the LIVING ECK MASTER from 1965 to 1971.

PLANE(S). The levels of existence, such as the Physical, Astral, Causal, Mental, Etheric, and Soul Planes.

REBAZAR TARZS. *REE-bah-zahr TAHRZ* A Tibetan ECK MASTER known as the torchbearer of ECKANKAR in the lower worlds.

SATSANG. *SAHT-sahng* A class in which students of ECK study a monthly lesson from ECKANKAR.

SELF-REALIZATION. SOUL recognition. The entering of Soul into the Soul PLANE and there beholding Itself as pure Spirit. A state of seeing, knowing, and being.

THE SHARIYAT-KI-SUGMAD. *SHAH-ree-aht-kee-SOOG-mahd* The sacred scriptures of ECKANKAR. The scriptures are comprised of about twelve volumes in the spiritual worlds. The first two were transcribed from the inner PLANES by PAUL TWITCHELL, modern-day founder of ECKANKAR.

SOUL. The True Self. The inner, most sacred part of each person. Soul exists before birth and lives on after the death of the physical body. As a spark of God, Soul can see, know, and perceive all things. It is the creative center of Its own world.

SOUL TRAVEL. The expansion of consciousness. The ability of SOUL to transcend the physical body and travel into the spiritual worlds of God. Soul Travel is taught only by the LIVING ECK MASTER. It helps people unfold spiritually and can provide proof of the existence of God and life after death.

SOUND AND LIGHT OF ECK. The Holy Spirit. The two aspects through which God appears in the lower worlds. People can experience them by looking and listening within themselves and through SOUL TRAVEL.

SPIRITUAL EXERCISES OF ECK. The daily practice of certain techniques to get us in touch with the Light and Sound of God.

SRI. *SREE* A title of spiritual respect, similar to reverend or pastor, used for those who have attained the Kingdom of God. In ECKANKAR, it is reserved for the MAHANTA, the LIVING ECK MASTER.

SUGMAD. *SOOG-mahd* A sacred name for God. Sugmad is neither masculine nor feminine; It is the source of all life.

TEMPLE(S) OF GOLDEN WISDOM. These Golden Wisdom Temples are spiritual temples which exist on the various PLANES—from the Physical to the Anami Lok; CHELAS of ECKANKAR are taken to the temples in the SOUL body to be educated in the divine knowledge; the different sections of the SHARIYAT-KI-SUGMAD, the sacred teachings of ECK, are kept at these temples.

TWITCHELL, PAUL. An American ECK MASTER who brought the modern teachings of ECKANKAR to the world through his writings and lectures. His spiritual name is PEDDAR ZASKQ.

VAIRAG. *vie-RAHG* Detachment.

WAH Z. *WAH zee* The spiritual name of SRI HAROLD KLEMP. It means the Secret Doctrine. It is his name in the spiritual worlds.

For more explanations of ECKANKAR terms, see *A Cosmic Sea of Words: The ECKANKAR Lexicon* by Harold Klemp.

BIBLIOGRAPHY

"Approaching the Temple." The Wisdom Notes, Vol. 23, No. 4, Winter 1990

"Are You Willing to Serve All Life?" The Wisdom Notes, Vol. 23, No. 1, Spring 1990

"An Awakened Consciousness." The Wisdom Notes, Vol. 18, No. 4, Winter 1985

"Awe of the Mind." The Wisdom Notes, Vol. 18, No. 1, Spring 1985

"Brushing Your Obstacles Aside." The Wisdom Notes, Vol. 16, No. 2, Spring 1983

"Community in Spirit." The Wisdom Notes, Vol. 22, No. 2, Summer 1989

"The Discipline of Love." The Wisdom Notes, Vol. 20, No. 4, Winter 1987

"Do You Follow Love or Power?" The Wisdom Notes, Vol. 18, No. 3, Fall 1985

"Endings Are Beginnings." The Wisdom Notes, Vol. 19, No. 3, Fall 1986

"Finding Success in ECK." The Wisdom Notes, Vol. 24, No. 1, Spring 1991

"Getting Past Spiritual Stagnation." The Wisdom Notes, Vol. 16, No. 1, January–February 1983

"Gifts of Healing." The Wisdom Notes, Vol. 19, No. 4, Winter 1986

"Going Home to God." The Wisdom Notes, Vol. 17, No. 1, Spring 1984

"How Love Enters the Heart." The Wisdom Notes, Vol. 23, No. 3, Fall 1990

"How to Be the HU." The Wisdom Notes, Vol. 25, No. 1, Spring 1992

"How to Open the Door Inside You." The Wisdom Notes, Vol. 15, No. 4, July–August 1982

"Insight from the Essence of God." The Wisdom Notes, Vol. 16, No. 3, Summer 1983

"Letting the ECK Heal You." The Wisdom Notes, Vol. 17, No. 3, Fall 1984

"Life Is Simply Change." The Wisdom Notes, Vol. 20, No. 1, Spring 1987

"Living Divine Love." The Wisdom Notes, Vol. 24, No. 4, Winter 1991

"The Long Road to God Consciousness." The Wisdom Notes, Vol. 20, No. 3, Fall 1987

"Loopholes for Locked Consciousness." The Wisdom Notes, Vol. 16, No. 4, Fall 1983

"Losses of the Heart." The Wisdom Notes, Vol. 18, No. 2, Summer 1985

"Love's Different Levels." The Wisdom Notes, Vol. 21, No. 1, Spring 1988

"Our New Spiritual Direction." The Wisdom Notes, Vol. 21, No. 3, Fall 1988

"Outer Answers to Inner Questions." The Wisdom Notes, Vol. 15, No. 5, September–October 1982

"Passing the Rod of ECK Power." The Wisdom Notes, Vol. 16, No. 5, Winter 1983

"A Passion for Truth." The Wisdom Notes, Vol. 21, No. 2, Summer 1988

"Right Action." The Wisdom Notes, Vol. 24, No. 3, Fall 1991

"Soul's Uniqueness." The Wisdom Notes, Vol. 20, No. 2, Summer 1987

"Spiritual Grace." The Wisdom Notes, Vol. 22, No. 3, Fall 1989

"Spiritual Showers." The Wisdom Notes, Vol. 17, No. 4, Winter 1984

"Stay or Go?" The Wisdom Notes, Vol. 19, No. 1, Spring 1986

"Through Testing Times." The Wisdom Notes, Vol. 17, No. 2, Summer 1984

"A True Understanding of Worship." The Wisdom Notes, Vol. 22, No. 4, Winter 1989

"Understanding Death." The Wisdom Notes, Vol. 19, No. 2, Summer 1986

"What Keeps You from God." The Wisdom Notes, Vol. 23, No. 2, Summer 1990

"What's the Lesson Here?" The Wisdom Notes, Vol. 22, No. 1, Spring 1989

"What We Preach and What We Practice." The Wisdom Notes, Vol. 24, No. 2, Summer 1991

"Where You Fit In, in ECK." The Wisdom Notes, Vol. 21, No. 4, Winter 1988

"Who Is Your Master?" The Wisdom Notes, Vol. 15, No. 2, March–April 1982

"Why Soul Is in the Lower Worlds." The Wisdom Notes, Vol. 15, No. 3, May–June 1982

"Your Spiritual Thirst." The Wisdom Notes, Vol. 15, No. 6, November–December 1982

INDEX

Churchmen, 181
Colors, 109
Columbus, 96
Comfort(s), 16, 129, 131
Commitment, 184
Common sense, 196
Community
  ECK, 8, 79, 81
  go into your, 48, 49
  of seekers, 9
  spiritual, 81, 184
Compassion, 48, 61–62
Confidence, 11, 27, 58, 109
Consciousness, 11. *See also*
    Cosmic consciousness; God
    Conscious(ness); Mahanta:
    Consciousness
  changing, 24
  expansion of, 76, 85, 96,
    150–51, 197, 207
  full, 216
  get-rich-quick, 35, 36
  of the God State, 180
  group, 54
  higher, 85, 120
  human, 7, 16, 24, 180, 192, 217
  individual units of, 83, 86
  in the inner worlds, 114
  levels of, 94
  living for, 34
  locked-in, 132, 184
  lower, 18
  Master not descending in, 158
  new, 165, 166, 183
  nondimensional, 95
  opening, 197
  of others, 126
  physical, 94
  of the public, 117
  temple of, 221
Construction worker(s), 3–4, 91
Contemplation. *See also* Spiritual
    Exercises of ECK;
    Technique(s)
  asking a question in, 33, 163,
    193, 195
  energy for, 96
  experience in, 33–34, 167, 180

  forms of, 60–61
  guidance through, 28, 50
  investigate your path through,
    221
  instead of meditation, 71, 192
  not overdoing, 49
  preparation for, 8
  psychic attack in, 176
  in Satsang class, 95, 208
  spend time each day in, 152
  time for, 48, 127
  using Light in, 159–60
  as worship, 127
Control, 43, 45
Cooperation, 92
Coronado, 173
Cosmic consciousness, 60
Cosmic Current, 182
Council of Nine, 197
Courage, 12, 184
Co-worker(s) with God
  as destiny of Soul, 71, 221
  future, 98
  as highest state, 80
  need to become a, 145
  as our mission, 50, 125
  your mission as, 145
Co-worker with the Mahanta,
    141
Creation(s), 83, 114, 162, 184,
    199
Creative arts, 97
Cremation, 113
Crisis, 48, 96
Cumberland Gap, 184
Cycle(s), 4, 152, 192

Death, 5, 117–20, 135–36, 196.
    See also Angel of Death;
    Fear(s): of death; King of the
    Dead; Near-death experi-
    ence; Translation; Yama
    Dutas
Decates, 219
Deceit, 18
Decision(s), 60, 86, 174
Dedication, ix, 141, 143, 147, 148
Deed(s), 18, 77

253

254

FOR FURTHER READING AND STUDY

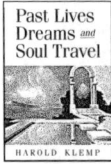

Past Lives, Dreams, and Soul Travel
Harold Klemp

What if you could recall past-life lessons for your benefit today? What if you could learn the secret knowledge of dreams to gain the wisdom of the heart? Or Soul Travel, to master the shift in consciousness needed to find peace and contentment? To ride the waves of God's love and mercy? Let Harold Klemp, leading authority in all three fields, show you how.

How to Survive Spiritually in Our Times, Mahanta Transcripts, Book 16
Harold Klemp

A master storyteller, Harold Klemp weaves stories, tips, and techniques into the golden fabric of his talks. They highlight the deeper truths within you, so you can apply them in your life *now*. He speaks right to Soul. It is that divine, eternal spark that you are. The survivor. Yet survival is only the starting point in your spiritual life. Harold Klemp also shows you how to gain in spiritual wealth. This book's a treasure.

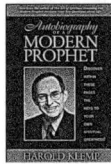

Autobiography of a Modern Prophet
Harold Klemp

Master your true destiny. Learn how this man's journey to God illuminates the way for you too. Dare to explore the outer limits of the last great frontier, your spiritual worlds! The more you explore them, the sooner you come to discovering your true nature as an infinite, eternal spark of God. This book helps you get there! A great read.

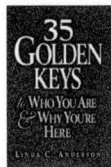

35 Golden Keys to Who You Are & Why You're Here
Linda C. Anderson

Discover thirty-five golden keys to mastering your spiritual destiny through the ancient teachings of Eckankar. The dramatic, true stories in this book equal anything found in the spiritual literature of today. Learn ways to immediately bring more love, peace, and purpose to your life. This book is an excellent introduction to Eckankar, the Mahanta, and the Mahanta Transcripts.

Available at your local bookstore. If unavailable, call (952) 380-2222. Or write: ECKANKAR, Dept. BK51, P.O. Box 27300, Minneapolis, MN 55427 U.S.A.

THERE MAY BE AN
ECKANKAR STUDY GROUP NEAR YOU

Eckankar offers a variety of local and international activities for the spiritual seeker. With hundreds of study groups worldwide, Eckankar is near you! Many areas have Eckankar centers where you can browse through the books in a quiet, unpressured environment, talk with others who share an interest in this ancient teaching, and attend beginning discussion classes on how to gain the attributes of Soul: wisdom, power, love, and freedom.

Around the world, Eckankar study groups offer special one-day or weekend seminars on the basic teachings of Eckankar. For membership information, visit the Eckankar Web site (www.eckankar.org). For the location of the Eckankar center or study group nearest you, click on "Other Eckankar Web sites" for a listing of those areas with Web sites. You're also welcome to check your phone book under **ECKANKAR**; call **(952) 380-2222, Ext. BK51;** or write **ECKANKAR, Att: Information, BK51, P.O. Box 27300, Minneapolis, MN 55427 U.S.A.**

☐ Please send me information on the nearest Eckankar center or study group in my area.

☐ Please send me more information about membership in Eckankar, which includes a twelve-month spiritual study.

Please type or print clearly

Name _____
     first (given)   last (family)

Street _____ Apt. # _____

City _____ State/Prov. _____

Zip/Postal Code _____ Country _____

ABOUT THE AUTHOR

Harold Klemp was born in Wisconsin and grew up on a small farm. He attended a two-room country schoolhouse before going to high school at a religious boarding school in Milwaukee, Wisconsin.

After preministerial college in Milwaukee and Fort Wayne, Indiana, he enlisted in the U.S. Air Force. There he trained as a language specialist at Indiana University and a radio intercept operator at Goodfellow AFB, Texas. Then followed a two-year stint in Japan where he first encountered Eckankar.

In October 1981, he became the spiritual leader of Eckankar, Religion of the Light and Sound of God. His full title is Sri Harold Klemp, the Mahanta, the Living ECK Master. As the Living ECK Master, Harold Klemp is responsible for the continued evolution of the Eckankar teachings.

His mission is to help people find their way back to God in this life. Harold Klemp travels to ECK seminars in North America, Europe, and the South Pacific. He has also visited Africa and many countries throughout the world, meeting with spiritual seekers and giving inspirational talks. There are many videocassettes and audiocassettes of his public talks available.

In his talks and writings, Harold Klemp's sense of humor and practical approach to spirituality have helped many people around the world find truth in their lives and greater inner freedom, wisdom, and love.

International Who's Who of Intellectuals
Ninth Edition

Reprinted with permission of Melrose Press Ltd.,
Cambridge, England, excerpted from *International Who's Who of
Intellectuals, Ninth Edition,* Copyright 1992
by Melrose Press Ltd.